"Most believers spend th[e] world. What a waste! All t[he] world. This book will open y[our] ... spiritual eyes to the natural[...] supernatural!"

Sid Roth, host, *It's Supernatural*

"In *Experiencing the Supernatural*, Rabbi K. A. Schneider challenges us to raise our expectations regarding the supernatural. This book will deepen your relationship with God."

Jentezen Franklin, senior pastor, Free Chapel;
New York Times bestselling author

"After 37 years of walking with God, I have learned the same lesson time again and again—all that matters in the end is spending time in the power and presence of God! This book is must-reading if you want to grow in your relationship with the Lord!"

Rabbi Jonathan Bernis, president and CEO,
Jewish Voice Ministries International

"Wow! What an eye-opener! Rabbi Schneider simply reverses your thinking. He teaches how to live in the supernatural from the inside and not from the outside. This is a must-read to learn how to train your senses to follow the witness of the Holy Spirit."

Marcus D. Lamb, founder/president,
Daystar Television Network

"I can honestly say after knowing Rabbi Schneider for many years that *Experiencing the Supernatural* exemplifies his walk with the living Savior! I have always been impressed by his love for God and his supernatural journey, which began at twenty after a visitation with Yeshua. If you desire to experience a realm where all things are possible, this is a must-read!"

Bishop Wayne Jackson, founder/president,
Impact Television Network

EXPERIENCING THE SUPERNATURAL

How to Saturate Your Life with the Power and Presence of God

MESSIANIC RABBI
K. A. SCHNEIDER

Chosen
a division of Baker Publishing Group
Minneapolis, Minnesota

© 2017 by Rabbi Kirt A. Schneider

Published by Chosen Books
11400 Hampshire Avenue South
Bloomington, Minnesota 55438
www.chosenbooks.com

Chosen Books is a division of
Baker Publishing Group, Grand Rapids, Michigan

Printed in the United States of America

Library of Congress Control Number: 2017941811

ISBN 978-0-8007-9837-6

Unless otherwise indicated, Scripture quotations are from the New American Standard Bible®, copyright © 1960, 1962, 1963, 1968, 1971, 1972, 1973, 1975, 1977, 1995 by The Lockman Foundation. Used by permission. (www.Lockman.org)

Scripture quotations identified KJV are from the King James Version of the Bible.

Cover design by LOOK Design

17 18 19 20 21 22 23   7 6 5 4 3 2 1

Contents

Contents

Foreword

In the modern world, we often learn from teachers who understand their subjects only on a theoretical level—who have lots of academic knowledge but no firsthand experience. I had a teacher like this in a university entrepreneurship class. He began the semester by announcing that he had never started a business before, but now he was going to teach us how to do it.

This is not the kind of teacher Jesus was. In fact, for Jesus, the demonstration did not follow the teaching; the demonstration actually came first!

Luke 24:19 says that Jesus was "a prophet mighty in deed and word" (KJV). To an English speaker, it sounds strange to put those words in that order. We would say "word and deed." But Luke's gospel clearly puts the actions before the words. In Acts 1:1 Luke talks about "all that Jesus began both to do and teach" (KJV). Again the demonstration comes first and the explanation follows. Jesus *taught* His students to help them understand what they first saw Him *do*. But the sad truth is that most missed it—as they do today. Most looked right at Jesus and completely misinterpreted what He was doing and what He was saying.

And what exactly was He doing? Acts 10:38 declares it plainly: "God anointed Jesus of Nazareth with the Holy Ghost and with power: [He] went about doing good, and healing all that were oppressed of the devil; for God was with him" (KJV)

Likewise, Jesus sent the disciples out with this commission: "And as ye go, preach, saying, the kingdom of heaven is at hand. Heal the sick, cleanse the lepers, raise the dead, cast out devils: freely ye have received, freely give" (Matthew 10:7–8 KJV).

We must not overlook this crystal-clear truth. When God's Kingdom comes, it must look like something. It must have a tangible demonstration. God's dominion is no ethereal, theoretical philosophy with no real-world consequences. When the Kingdom of heaven collides with the natural world, there is visible, demonstrable evidence of God's dominion—for example, the sick are healed, the lepers are cleansed, the dead are raised, the power of Satan is broken, and the oppressed are freed!

Some think mistakenly that Jesus' miracles simply proved that He was the Messiah. How convenient that would be for us! If the miracles of Jesus were merely proof of his Messianic claims, we are off the hook. But this is simply not the case. Jesus' miracles were more than evidence of His role; they were actually demonstrations that imply *our* role.

Jesus performs mighty miracles, for example, in Matthew 12. He heals a man with a withered hand (verse 13). Then He heals a demonized, blind and mute man so that he can speak and see (verse 22). In fact, verse 15 tells us that "great multitudes followed him, and *he healed them all*" (KJV, emphasis added). But here is the amazing part: Just a few verses later, the scribes and Pharisees still insist, "We want to see a sign from You" (verse 38 NASB)! Can you imagine such nerve? They have just seen that every single sickness, every disease and every infirmity among a great multitude of people was healed! I know of no greater demonstration in history of the miraculous. But Jesus' critics are not impressed or convinced.

These miracles were not the kind of "signs" the doubters sought. They wanted something more spectacular, more grandiose. They wanted Jesus to part the sea like Moses or call down fire from heaven like Elijah. Jesus would eventually give them that kind of sign—His resurrection from the dead—and still they would not believe (see Matthew 12:39–40). But in the meantime His healings and miracles were not attempts to prove something to the skeptics. Rather, *they were demonstrations of what it looks like when a human being walks in Kingdom dominion.* In other words, Jesus did not perform miracles to prove that He could. He performed miracles to prove that *we* could. He was saying, "Look! This is the Kingdom I have been teaching you about. This is what it looks like when it comes to earth. This is what I want *you* to do."

But there is a problem. Fallen humans cannot walk in Kingdom dominion. We are dead in trespasses and sins. We are under the curse and controlled by the powers of the air (see Ephesians 2:1–3). That is why Jesus not only demonstrated and taught the Kingdom; He also died to give the Kingdom to those who believe (see Luke 12:32). His death on the cross was not simply to rescue us from hell; it was to restore the dominion we lost in the Garden.

And so much more. It was to make us kings and priests to God. It was to restore the purpose and calling God placed on the human race since the beginning of time. It was for us to subdue the earth and take dominion—not simply over plants and animals, but over "serpents and scorpions, and over all the power of the enemy" (Luke 10:19 KJV). He died so that we could live the same way He lived. Jesus did not die just to get us into heaven. He died to get heaven into us and through us into the fallen world.

The supernatural is not some incidental and occasional "cherry on top" of the Christian life. It *is* the Christian life. Salvation itself is an unfathomable miracle. If Christians are born of the Spirit, they are by definition supernatural creatures. How can they not live supernatural lives? For any believer who dares to take the Scriptures seriously, there is no escaping this indisputable conclusion: Christians are supposed to live the miraculous life every day. The question is, How?

In his new book, *Experiencing the Supernatural*, Rabbi Schneider uses his powerful testimony to unveil how this kind of supernatural life is possible. More importantly, by giving tools and keys from his own experience, he demystifies the miraculous, making it practical as well.

In *Experiencing the Supernatural*, Rabbi Schneider delves into the supernatural mindset, learning to wait on God, living life through the Spirit, and much more. This book is not a collection of untried theories. It is a word of wisdom from a man who has experienced the supernatural in his life. It is an invitation to begin *Experiencing the Supernatural* in your own life.

Daniel Kolenda, missionary evangelist and bestselling author

PART 1

Discovering Mysteries

1

The Mystery of the Ages

When I was a young Jewish guy growing up in Cleveland, Ohio, I never thought about Jesus one way or the other. He was a nonissue. I was bar mitzvahed in a conservative temple in one of the strongest Jewish communities in the nation, and, although I was lost and without hope, I did not know Jesus from anything.

But one night when I was twenty years old, as I was lying in my bed, the Lord awakened me from sleep. Suddenly I was supernaturally aware that I was surrounded by a supernatural presence. I had supernatural consciousness. And in that state Jesus appeared to me on the cross in a vision. I could see the terrain and people looking at Him from a distance.

Then, in the vision, a ray of red light shone straight through the sky and beamed down on Yeshua's head. When I saw that ray of red light coming from straight above, I knew it was coming from God. God was telling me that Jesus was the way to Him. Jesus was revealing Himself to me as the Messiah.

As an American I knew enough to know the Person on the cross was Jesus, and *bam*, I got saved. I jumped out of bed and looked at my clock radio—it was 3:30 in the morning. I was excited. I had never thought about supernatural things. In the days that followed, I began looking everywhere for God. I was charged up about what had happened. I knew Yeshua was alive. I knew He was real. I knew I could experience His supernatural reality, and this became my goal in life.

I started going to churches all over the city, searching for answers. Wherever a meeting was going on, I was there. And I did everything I was told to do. I could not have read my new Bible any more than I was reading it. I could not have prayed any longer than I was praying. I could not have given any more money than I was giving. I could not have witnessed to any more people than I was witnessing to. If you were behind me in line at the grocery store, I would have turned around and witnessed to you. I witnessed to everybody. I was doing all those things, and those are things we should be doing, but I was looking for God and His supernatural power in the wrong place.

After I pressed along that path for ten years, God finally spoke to me. He said, *The reason you're not finding what you're looking for is that you're looking for Me on the outside. You don't understand that I'm already in you.*

God had shown Himself to me supernaturally, but I was trying to experience His power and presence in the outside natural world—in the things I could touch and see. I wanted to fill my life with God's power, but I made little progress. I was looking for God in my works and in specific places that were outside of myself. That is why I went to Christian gatherings almost every night of the week all over the city of Cleveland, hoping to find what I was looking for in those meetings and then doing everything they told me to do. Doing Christian works and attending Spirit-filled meetings are good things to be involved in, but, ultimately, until we understand that God is in us, we will not have supernatural peace. And this is true of most Christians. We want the supernatural to be part of our everyday lives—we hope to pray effectively for healing, to rout demons, to understand dreams and visions, to catch the signs of His leading—but sadly we miss most of it. We expect the supernatural to be found in the world around us, yet we wind up frustrated, disillusioned or burnt out.

Yeshua said that a person's life does not consist in an abundance of "things." You and I will never become satisfied by trying to find Him in more and more possessions or titles or religious trophies—things that are outside ourselves. The only time we will find peace is when we understand that Messiah Yeshua is in us. That is why Jesus cautioned, "If someone says to you, 'Look! There's the Kingdom' or 'Look over there! There's the Kingdom,' don't run there. The Kingdom of God is within you."

God has given us His Spirit to reveal Himself to us. The Bible says, "'Things which eye has not seen and ear has not heard, and which have not entered the heart of man, all that God has prepared for those who love Him.' For to us God revealed them through the Spirit; for the Spirit searches all things, even the depths of God" (1 Corinthians 2:9–10). His Spirit is in us. He wants us to come into a relationship of intimacy with Him and of identity with Him. The same power that raised Yeshua from the dead resides in every born-again believer. When we begin to grasp this, we come to a place of foundational peace and strength and power.

15

It Starts with a Change of Focus

Believers, as a whole, have a great deal of misunderstanding regarding this concept of God's Spirit dwelling inside us. Spirit, by definition, operates outside the laws of the natural world, but believers seem to spend much of their time looking for God *in* the natural world. That is why we miss so much of the supernatural experience.

Think of it this way. God who is Spirit created the visible world. Should we take our cues, then, from the created things around us—or from the Spirit who created them?

When Peter saw Jesus walking on the water, he said, "Lord, call me to come."

Jesus said, "Come."

Sometimes like Peter we say yes. We grasp the concept that Jesus is the higher reality, and we walk in the power of the Spirit. But let me ask you a question, and I ask myself the same question: Are we always living as though His Word is superior and supersedes and reigns above the visible world? No. We do what Peter did next. He believed, but then he looked at the waves. He gave greater credence to the visible world. He lost his grip on the supernatural reality and sank down into the natural.

We need to learn to walk by faith and not by sight, feelings or our own thoughts. When God revealed to me that I was not finding Him because I was looking for Him on the outside and in my works, a major transition began for me. In fact, from that moment to this day, power came into my life that I had not previously experienced.

It was a great shifting. I stopped running all over the place and simply sat before Him, resting in His presence, asking Him to help me become aware that the supernatural expression of His Kingdom starts with His presence within my own heart. I am not waiting until I die and go to heaven to move in the supernatural. God has revealed Himself to us here on earth, and I believe that we can saturate our lives with a sense of His power and presence.

The Mystery Revealed

This concept of Messiah living inside us was prophesied in the Hebrew Bible. Jeremiah 31:33 and Ezekiel 36:24–28 speak of God putting His Law and His Spirit within us. God foretold through the prophet Joel that He was going to "pour out" His Spirit upon humankind (Joel 2:28). In Yeshua, this plan moved into completion; the mystery of the ages—meaning the hidden message of the Scriptures going all the way back to the beginning—was finally revealed.

It took place with the institution of the New Covenant when Yeshua celebrated Passover with His disciples and lifted up that cup of Passover wine. When He said, "This is My blood shed for you in the New Covenant," He was inaugurating two things.

Number one, final atonement for sin was going to be made with His death on the cross. You recall that in the Old Covenant, God's people had to keep offering up the sacrifices day after day, year after year. Those sacrifices were simply shadows of the one ultimate sacrifice. It has now been revealed that the final payment for sin—past, present and future sin, once and for all—has been made through the Person of Jesus, God Himself in the flesh.

The second thing that Jesus inaugurated at that Passover meal was God moving from the outside to the inside. You see, in the Old Covenant, God dealt with people mostly from the outside. When people wanted to meet God, for instance, they went to a specific place such as the Temple in Jerusalem. God's presence dwelt literally in the Holy of Holies above the Ark of the Covenant between the two cherubim on the mercy seat in the Temple. When Yeshua was crucified, however, the veil separating the Holy of Holies from the world was torn in half (see Matthew 27:51). God was showing that now all humankind has access to Him. Then God poured His Spirit upon all flesh (see Acts 2:1–21)!

God no longer dwells in the Temple. He has moved from the outside to the inside. Through Jesus all of us are invited to become recipients of His Spirit, to receive Him into ourselves—to be born again. What greater gift can we possibly receive than the gift of God Himself? Yet that is what we have been given.

This is the mystery of the ages that Paul said has now been disclosed to the Lord's people (see Colossians 1:26–27). The message is this: Messiah is in you, and He is your hope of glory. When you become a recipient of the Spirit of God Himself, you become partaker of the divine nature. This is why John wrote that believers are called the children of God, because we have received His very Spirit.

If you are born again, God has literally put His Spirit inside you—Yeshua, Jesus Himself, in the Person of His Spirit lives in you. He wants to draw you out of the world to Himself.

A Light in the Temple

The Hebrew Bible also gives us a pattern for this life of supernatural experience. In the book of Exodus we read that God told His people to build a Mishkan, a Tabernacle, so He could dwell among them and have fellowship with them: "Let them construct a sanctuary for Me, that I may dwell among them. According to all that I am going to show you, as the pattern of the tabernacle and the pattern of all its furniture, just so you shall construct it" (Exodus 25:8–9). The Lord, Yahweh Himself, designed the Tabernacle so He could have intimacy with His people. Every part of that Tabernacle was there for a reason.

Before entering the Tabernacle, you passed the brazen altar of burnt offering where you received forgiveness of sins, then the brass laver, which speaks of being cleansed. Then you entered into the Holy Place, and the first thing you probably noticed, because of the light coming from it, was the golden lampstand.

This lampstand, or menorah, was made of one piece of pure, hammered gold. The center stem and six branches, three extending from each side, held seven oil lamps. The Holy Place was covered with animal skins, so no light was present except that which shone from the lamps.

This has direct connection to the New Covenant and the Lord's greeting to the churches. He begins, "Grace to you and peace, from Him who is and who was and who is to come; and from the seven Spirits who are before His throne" (Revelation 1:4). The Lord is speaking of the Holy Spirit, the *Ruach HaKodesh*. He is not talking about seven individual, disconnected spirits, but rather the sevenfold manifestation of the Holy Spirit. That is why the menorah in the Tabernacle, and later in the Temple, was made from one piece of pure gold with seven lamps.

This menorah was a symbol of the light of the Holy Spirit. And the only way you could perceive the things of God inside the Holy Place—the altar of incense and the table of showbread that were in the Holy Place—was through the light of the menorah.

It is also true that the only way you and I can perceive the things of God is through the light of the Holy Spirit. If we want to live by natural light, we can go outside the Tabernacle and live by the light of the sun. But if we want to live by God's light, we must rely on the light of His Spirit.

God wants us to become more dependent upon His Spirit, the *Ruach HaKodesh*. God wants to draw us back to Himself. He wants us to take a simpler approach to Him. No one has to be an expert in Hebrew or Greek or strive harder or work longer. We just have to come before Him and rely on His Spirit.

You see, the disciples of Jesus were uneducated men, and yet they knew Him intimately. They did not have complete Bibles such as you and I have today, but they did have the Spirit of God. We do not have to be rocket scientists to figure this out. We simply have to be humble, to depend on Him and to receive life from Him through His Holy Spirit.

As we move into our discovery of what it means to experience the supernatural, start looking for any ways in which God might be leading you to reposition yourself spiritually. Be aware of how you are looking for God in an outer experience—whether it be religion, works, study, politics, socializing or some other avenue to fulfillment. There is nothing wrong with any of these, but you cannot find God in them.

I am going to help you discover a plan that, when applied, will lead you into this reality that His Spirit is within you. Jesus wants you to walk in the power of the Spirit. He wants you to experience the supernatural. In fact, unless you and I expect the supernatural in our relationships with God, we cannot truly walk with Him. To have this deeper relationship and experience with God, let's begin by developing conscious awareness of the Holy Spirit in us, which leads to a supernatural mindset.

2

Developing a
Supernatural Mindset

God created us to have dominion over this world. One of our greatest hindrances to living in this victory is that we let Satan draw us out of God's close presence. Too many times we go running off in search of the supernatural in the world around us, chasing after a multitude of things that we hope will get us there, but the effort leads only to frustration and, in some cases, darkness. Since Satan's deception is aided by the culture we live in, we rarely even recognize what is happening.

Contrast that experience with the calm understanding that God is supernaturally within us. As our lives become saturated with His power and presence, we begin to expect the supernatural to be at work in us. Not only do we acknowledge what Jesus has done, but we also bring that finished work into our everyday experiences. We refuse to live as victims of the physical universe or the enemy's deceptions; rather, we learn to exercise dominion in this physical world. In other words, the supernatural becomes natural to us.

The mystery of the ages has been revealed: The Son of God lives in us, literally, by the power of the Holy Spirit. With the understanding that He wants to draw us out of the world into Himself, we can begin to develop a supernatural mindset. This is not just a mental exercise. A supernatural mindset does not mean only believing in the supernatural. Many people believe in the supernatural. A supernatural mindset comes by *walking in and experiencing* the supernatural in our lives. Let's explore key applications that help us put this into practice, beginning with safeguards for any supernatural experience.

Marriage of Word and Spirit

A lot of people are interested in the spirit world, so how do we know that we are following the right spirit? It begins with the Word of God. The Word of God is living and active and sharper than a two-edged sword, for it divides even soul and spirit. If we are not anchored in the Word, we will be deceived. There is no question about it. We will be deceived predominately by Satan, who disguises himself as an angel of light, and by all the supernatural things he is able to do.

Have you ever had a supernatural phenomenon, a supernatural "sign" that you thought was from God but turned out to be a counterfeit sign from Satan who was trying to deceive you to go the wrong way? Most of us have.

A young friend of mine who is in ministry was praying for a wife. At one point he heard a performance by a Christian musician, whom I will call Mary, whose music touched him. He thought, *Maybe she is to be my wife.*

He went to bed with his TV on and in the middle of the night he was awakened to hear the voice of a preacher saying, "And God chose Mary." Now he was really attentive to this, thinking that God was giving him a sign that this woman was to be his wife. This was followed by many other "supernatural" signs—such as a dream that he and Mary were forming a relationship—to the point that he became one hundred percent certain that she was the one. Before long, he heard that Mary was engaged to another man, but this did not deter him. He thought, *Well, they aren't married yet!* He decided that God was able to change her course.

Due to the circumstances, I cautioned him about buying in to all the supposed signs—not to mention the fact that he had never even met Mary! But he was convinced. He told me, and others who tried to warn him, that if he was wrong about this, he did not know God at all.

Well, as it turned out, Mary married the man she was engaged to. Fortunately, my friend was not as broken about it as I was concerned he might be. He said that at first it felt like a punch in the stomach—not because she would not be his wife, but because he thought he could not trust God's voice for direction. In time he saw how God used it to teach him that he was depending too heavily on emotions, feelings and even signs to get direction for life.

A lot of people go through much the same thing. In fact, I have seen many young people be misled with false supernatural signs when looking too eagerly for a mate. Satan knows when a person is desperate for something. The point is that not every sign comes from the Spirit of God.

My friend missed the balance of Word and Spirit: The Word says to pay attention to the godly counsel of the spiritual people God has placed in one's life; and the Holy Spirit will never lead in a way contrary to the written Word. Remember that Pharaoh's magicians were able to perform supernatural signs with their staffs—and the devil's deception did not cease with them. Jesus predicted so many false signs and wonders taking place in the spiritual world at the end of the age that, if it were not for the grace of God, even the elect would be deceived. The written Word of God is the foundation for our faith— it defines all doctrine for life and conduct. We never deviate from it. If a thought or action cannot be backed by Scripture, then we throw out that thought or action.

There is a marriage between the Word of God and the Spirit of God. The Father is looking for those who will walk with Him: "God is spirit, and those who worship Him must worship in spirit and truth" (John 4:24). Those interested only in spiritual experiences open themselves to deception. There are many spirits. We need God's Word, His truth, to keep us on the straight and narrow path that leads to life. Jesus said, "The words that I have spoken to you are spirit and are life" (John 6:63). Scripture, God's Word, gives us all the general parameters and instructions that we need for walking with God.

But what about the times we need specific individual direction? Everyone's life journey is different. The Spirit, according to the heart of Jesus, guides us through any specific concerns we have. He can speak to us in detail about any area where we need help—what person to date or marry, what job to take, where to live geographically, and many, many, many other practical issues.

It is only in the union of being led by the Word and led by the Spirit that we enter into the fullness of what Jesus has for us. The Spirit will not lead us into any action contrary to Scripture, and Scripture leads us to God but does not replace the work of God's Spirit. We need both!

That was the mistake the Pharisees made. They followed God's Law but made no room for God's Spirit. Jesus told them, "You search the Scriptures because you think in them you have life. The Scriptures are actually designed to lead you to Me, and yet you won't come to Me that you might have life" (see John 5:39–40).

The Word gives us general life guidelines, and the Spirit of the Lord leads us through the specific situations we encounter. The two work together. If we think the only means of grace that the Lord has given us for experiencing the supernatural is the Bible, then we are missing half the picture. The Bible is the foundation. The Spirit gives us the ability to know specifically how to make those decisions that are uniquely personal to us.

When I preach in evangelistic meetings in foreign countries, for example, I wait upon God for Him to show me what to preach. This comes by trusting Him and allowing the Spirit to put His burden on my heart. And often this does not happen until I step onto the platform and begin to preach. Because I spend a lot of time studying the written Word, I am able to merge the Scriptures that I have learned with the sense of what God's Spirit puts upon my heart to preach. This is an example of the marriage between the Spirit and the Word.

The Key to Understanding Scripture

Yeshua spoke this: "He who has my commandments and keeps them is the one who loves Me; and he who loves Me will be loved by My Father" (John 14:21). Without the Spirit giving us revelation for these words, it could sound as though the Father will love us based upon our works, based upon our ability to keep His commandments. When I read this

Scripture, it felt to me that God's love for me was not unconditional, but conditional—that only as I kept the Father's commandments would He love me.

Is this what Scripture is saying here? Notice verse 23 as Jesus continues on this theme: "If anyone loves Me, he will keep My word; and My Father will love him, and We will come to him and make Our abode with him."

Again, as I read this I was confused because everything else I had read in Scripture and had been taught was about God's unconditional love for me, whereas these verses seem to say that God's love is contingent upon my obedience and love for Him. This scared me—and it contradicted Romans 5:8, which says, "While we were yet sinners, Christ died for us." Jesus did not die for us because we love Him, but because He loves us.

As I pondered this, the Holy Spirit began to give me revelation about it. Finally I understood. Jesus is not talking specifically about giving His love to us; He is talking about releasing *the revelation* of His love for us.

His love never changes. He is never going to love you any more or any less than He does right now. But as you obey Him, as you seek Him, as you draw near to Him, as you begin to cultivate the knowledge of Yeshua in your heart, then God releases to you the revelation of how much He loves you. He begins to draw near to you, and He begins to make His presence with you felt.

We do not keep His commandments because we hope to earn salvation or become righteous or holy. We obey Jesus because we want to be one with Him. We want to get closer to Him. Obedience comes out of our yearning for closeness and fellowship with our God. It is as though Jesus is saying, "If you love Me so much that you obey Me, then I'm going to draw near to you and release to you the revelation of how much I love you. I'm going to give you revelation of who I am, and the Father and I will make Our abode with you." The point that I am trying to underscore here is the necessity not to rely on the Word only or, on the other hand, the Spirit only. We need to rely on both the Spirit and the Word together. Without the Spirit, we will misunderstand the Word just like the Pharisees. This is why understanding the marriage of Word and Spirit is crucial to a supernatural mindset.

Application Steps

Because God is supernatural, we must develop a supernatural mindset to walk with Him. Here are four foundational steps that can help you develop a supernatural mindset. Whether these are things you have contemplated in the past or are new concepts, let me encourage you to begin to practice them regularly. Paul said that bodily discipline is profitable because it yields benefits in this age, but spiritual discipline is even more profitable because it also yields dividends in the age to come (see 1 Timothy 4:8). These steps might be challenging, but remember: God wants you to succeed.

Step One: Come Out from the World

The first step is to separate yourself from whatever in the world lures you away from closeness with Yeshua. The Lord says, "Come out from the world. Draw near to me, and I will receive you to Myself" (see 2 Corinthians 6:17).

If you need to repent for seeking the things of the world more than you seek intimacy with God, then do so. Are there temptations in the world that you struggle with? Addictive habits or behaviors? Is television an addiction for you? Then come away from it. Christians should not be entertained by watching the very things that put Yeshua on the cross. What about workaholism? Shopaholism? Food? Secular music? Are you going to Facebook for answers every time you have a problem? Make a commitment to spend time with God (reading Scripture, devotionals and Christian books; listening to Christian music; etc.) that you would otherwise spend in some of these activities. A supernatural mindset is developed simply by coming out from the world and coming to Him. This includes taking your focus off the visible world to focus instead on His unseen reality.

The apostle John wrote: "All that is in the world, the lust of the flesh and the lust of the eyes and the boastful pride of life, is not from the Father, but is from the world" (1 John 2:16). For many, the greatest lure that brings us outside of the Spirit is the lust of the eyes and of the flesh that is related to our sexual makeup. It is natural to be attracted to members of the opposite sex, but Scripture is clear that this type of lust is not to be yielded to but is to be subdued.

Paul said, "Flee from youthful lusts" (2 Timothy 2:22.) We cannot abide in the Spirit and at the same time give ourselves over to sensual and earthly lusts. Scripture says, "The flesh sets its desire against the Spirit, and the Spirit against the flesh" (Galatians 5:17)—meaning that the two are opposed to each other. Paul also said, "If you are living according to the flesh, you must die; but if by the Spirit you are putting to death the deeds of the body, you will live" (Romans 8:13).

We are not going to ascend into the supernatural if we give ourselves over to the lust of the flesh. Through resisting the lust of the flesh, staying focused on God and abiding in His Spirit, we will ascend into the supernatural and develop a supernatural mindset.

Step Two: Stop Running

The second step is closely related: Stop running from your fears and insecurities.

We read in Genesis 3:7 that when Adam and Eve sinned, they realized that they were naked. That realization was the first effect we see of their sin. What does that mean? They were naked before and it did not bother them, but suddenly they felt exposed and it made them insecure and afraid. They tried to run from their nakedness and to cover it up with fig leaves, but because the fear was inside them, it was impossible to run from it.

All of us—by virtue of being born into a fallen world and having a sin nature—come to a place eventually where we begin to feel exposed, just as Adam and Eve did in the Garden. We get a feeling inside that something is not right, and we feel anxious and try to run from that feeling by going into the world, just as Adam and Eve did. As they tried to cover up their insecurity with the fig leaves, we, too, hope to find security and identity in material things. The problem is that the feeling of fear and insecurity can never really be left behind because wherever we go, there we are.

If this resonates with you, know that God wants you to be settled in His peace and grounded in Him. Stop running from your fears and insecurities, trying to cover them up with the things of the world. You can bring them to Him.

Step Three: Receive His Peace

It is through peace that we abide in the Lord and experience His supernatural presence in our everyday lives. Yeshua connected the gift of His Holy Spirit with peace: "My peace I give to you; not as the world gives do I give to you" (John 14:27). That is why Yeshua is called the Prince of Peace. This is who He is. This is why He was able to speak to the sea and still the storm. Because He had such inner peace, He was able to express it in dominion over the wind and waves.

We see this same phenomenon when Yeshua breathed on His disciples after His resurrection and said, "Shalom, peace be with you. Receive the Holy Spirit" (see John 20:21–22). When we receive the Holy Spirit, we receive an impartation of peace. And as we learn how to abide in the Holy Spirit, who is within us, we will become more and more settled. We will grow in our ability to be still and rest in the Lord. This brings wholeness.

Peace precedes authority. Peace precedes power. It is only in peace that you can discern the heart, the mind and the thoughts of God. God's shalom is inside you.

Step Four: Realize That God Wants to Rest in You!

Do you know that God wants you to become a habitation for Him? We read in Scripture about David wanting to build the Lord a house, a resting place (see 2 Samuel 7:1–2). Today believers are His house. His habitation is no longer a physical structure; we have become His resting place.

I think John 14:23 is one of the most beautiful sections in all the Bible. In this section of Scripture, which we talked about earlier, Yeshua speaks about how He wants to come to us and make His home within us: "If anyone loves Me, he will keep My word; and My Father will love him, and We will come to him and make Our abode with him." Yeshua wants to reveal Himself to us. He is not talking about a personal encounter in the life to come; He is talking about this life. He and the Father will make their abode with us, here and now. He wants to be at rest in our lives. He does not want us to be striving against Him—or Him against us. Having a supernatural mindset means that His thoughts become our thoughts; His will becomes our will. This enables Him to rest in us as His temple. As we overcome and bring our hearts and thoughts into harmony with God's heart and thoughts, He will be able to be at rest in us and we will find ourselves being made whole in Him.

Building Relationship

As you take these foundational steps toward developing a supernatural mindset, you will find an important change taking place in your heart. God will bring revelation to you about your identity. You will become more aware of who you are in and to Him. This is not an instantaneous process, but a growing process that takes place over time. And yet it is powerful and entirely supernatural. Everything is birthed out of relationship. When you and I know how much God loves us, we will walk in victory.

Satan, of course, does not want us to come into the full revelation of God's love. We see this principle in action even in the life of Yeshua. As soon as Yeshua was baptized and came up out of the Jordan River, the heavens opened, the Spirit of God descended in the form of a dove, and the voice spoke from heaven and said, "You are My beloved Son, in You I am well-pleased" (Luke 3:22). Then the devil showed up. Yeshua was led into the wilderness where He faced temptation by the devil to turn stones into bread, to throw Himself down from the Temple and to receive the splendor of the world by worshiping the evil one. But, you see, the real temptation was not for Jesus to act in a way that would test God. The real result Satan wanted was to make Yeshua question the Father's love for Him.

God the Father had just finished saying to Jesus, "You are My beloved Son." The devil knew that if he could take away Yeshua's confidence in His identity, he would win the battle. So the devil began, "*If* you are the Son of God . . ." There is the temptation. That is what Satan was after. To remove from Jesus the knowledge that He was God's beloved Son.

It is the same with you. God wants to give you identity in His love for you, but Satan wants to steal it. He hopes to succeed in his deception primarily by luring you away from God and by causing you to run in fear after the things of the world. This is why it is so important to have a supernatural mindset. If you hold to the foundation of the Word and spend time alone with Him every day to receive the Holy Spirit's revelation and encouragement, then you will be strong against the enemy's attacks.

God wants to reveal to you by His Spirit how much He loves you. He wants to give you revelation to know Him. He wants to strengthen you with the power that raised Jesus from the dead. He is saying, "Ask and it will be given to you. Draw near to Me, and I will draw near to you."

The book of Revelation tells us that "something like a sea of glass" is before the throne of God (Revelation 4:6). What does that mean? The sea of glass speaks of perfect and absolute stillness before the Lord's throne. No worry, no anxiety. No fear of the future. Perfect, still peace. And that is the peace that God has for you as you begin to saturate your life with His power and presence.

3

What God Reveals through the Jewish People

The supernatural mysteries of God are few places more evident than in His consistent faithfulness to His chosen people, the Jews. This helps the Church in her own experience of the supernatural in two important ways. Seeing God's faithfulness to Israel encourages all followers of Yeshua to believe that God will be faithful to each one of us. In addition, the supernatural anointing on the Jews comes on those who honor them.

A Secure Identity

I like the way Mark Twain contemplated the supernatural blessing of God on Israel in an essay printed in *Harper's Monthly* in 1898:

> The Egyptian, the Babylonian, and the Persians rose, filled the planet with sound and splendor, then faded to dream-stuff

and passed away; the Greek and the Roman followed, and made a vast noise, and they are gone; other peoples have sprung up and held their torch high for a time, but it burned out, and they sit in twilight now, or have vanished. The Jew saw them all, beat them all, and is now what he always was, exhibiting no decadence, no infirmities of age, no weakening of his parts, no slowing of his energies, no dulling of his alert and aggressive mind. All things are mortal but the Jew; all other forces pass, but he remains. What is the secret of his immortality?

How do we explain this? For some 2,700 years, *for two-thirds of their existence*, the Jewish people were driven out of their homeland to the outermost parts of the earth. Dispersed. Scattered. They were no longer united physically to each other but were rather absorbed into other nations. In dispersion they no longer even shared a common history. The Jews in Spain had one history. The Jews in Morocco had another history. The Jews in Russia had another history, and on it goes as far back as their ancient captivity by the Assyrians and Babylonians.

Then in one day, after being displaced for all that time, God gave them back their nation, and they began returning from all corners of the world to be united in their land. Supernaturally, on May 14, 1948, David Ben-Gurion proclaimed the reborn State of Israel.

But this still did not mean peaceful existence for God's people. The Jews were attacked immediately by their Arab neighbors, a combined coalition of forces from Egypt, Jordan, Syria, Lebanon and Iraq. Have you ever looked at Israel on a map and seen how small it is? It is about the size of the state of New Jersey. Compared to the size of the Arab nations around it, that is small. All of those nations came against Israel at once, and yet, remarkably, through a super-natural miracle, Israel not only survived but prevailed. And the nation that had seemingly perished was now alive and well. Even its language of Hebrew—a dead language—had been brought to life in a modern form so that today more than six million Jews in Israel have resumed speaking their native tongue.

In 1967 Israel again dealt with Arab aggressors, predomi-nantly Egypt, Syria and Jordan, in what is known as the Six-Day War. Israel not only survived, but it regained territory and recaptured the Old City of Jerusalem. And then came the Yom Kippur War in 1973. Egypt and Syria attacked Israel on the most holy day of the year when the Jewish people were worshiping. But what happened? Once again, a super-natural miracle. Israel continued to survive and to thrive. And on it goes.

Remarkably, through these many centuries of conflict, the Jewish people never lost their sense of identity. They held to their common memory—that nearly 3,500 years ago the Lord "passed over" their homes in Egypt, spared their firstborn sons, parted the Red Sea and delivered them from bondage. Every year since those miraculous events, Jews all over the world have continued the Passover celebration, holding fast to their supernatural destiny as God's chosen people—not forgetting who they are and why they are who they are.

Blessings Come from the Covenant

Along with the miracle of God's preserving Israel, Yahweh God has also blessed them with divine intelligence. The Jewish people make up only one-fifth of one percent of the core population of the world. And yet 22 percent of Nobel

Prize winners are Jews. They have risen to the top and have influence all over the earth. Science, medicine, technology, economics, business—Israel is a world leader in many fields. It is interesting that Israel leads the world in diamond cutting because that is who they are. They are a small people, but they are diamonds in the sight of God.

How could such a small race of people have such a disproportionate influence upon the world today? How do you explain this? You explain this because God made a covenant with them. This supernatural blessing on the Jewish people goes back to the promise God gave Abraham.

Genesis records the words of this promise:

> Now the LORD said to Abram, "Go forth from your country, and from your relatives and from your father's house, to the land which I will show you; and I will make you a great nation, and I will bless you, and make your name great; and so you shall be a blessing; and I will bless those who bless you, and the one who curses you I will curse. And in you all the families of the earth will be blessed."
>
> Genesis 12:1–3

This was repeated to Abraham when he offered up his son Isaac:

> "By Myself I have sworn, declares the LORD, because you have done this thing and have not withheld your son, your only son, indeed I will greatly bless you, and I will greatly multiply your seed as the stars in the heavens and as the sand which is on the seashore; and your seed shall possess the gate of their enemies. In your seed all the nations of the earth shall be blessed, because you have obeyed My voice."
>
> Genesis 22:16–18

The covenant blessings were often affirmed throughout Israel's early history, such as this declaration to Moses:

> "For you are a holy people to the LORD your God; the LORD your God has chosen you to be a people for His own possession out of all the peoples who are on the face of the earth. The LORD did not set His love on you nor choose you because you were more in number than any of the peoples, for you were the fewest of all peoples, but because the LORD loved you and kept the oath which He swore to your forefathers, the LORD brought you out by a mighty hand and redeemed you from the house of slavery, from the hand of Pharaoh king of Egypt."
>
> Deuteronomy 7:6–8

The Lord did not love and protect them because they were a large force but because He was keeping the covenant He had made with Abraham—not only that Israel would be preserved and blessed but also that in her seed all the nations would be blessed.

Out of Their Rejection

God's promise to Abraham to multiply his seed and to bless the world through these people is being fulfilled in two stages, which we see stated in Romans 11:15: "If their rejection [of their Messiah] is the reconciliation of the world, what will their acceptance be but life from the dead?" Let's look at the first stage, the first part of this verse.

Because of the Jews' rejection of the Gospel, Jesus' disciples began spreading the Good News to Gentiles all over the world. Think about Paul's journey. When Paul had the supernatural experience of meeting and receiving Jesus, he was sure God would use him to bring salvation to the Jews. He probably thought he was the perfect candidate to turn their hearts to their Messiah: *They know me—they know I am a Pharisee, educated by the leading sage of our day, Gamaliel. They know how I was opposed to any Jew who believed in Jesus. When I go tell them how Jesus really is the Messiah, how He appeared to me supernaturally, they will surely trust my testimony. Who could be a better witness to them than I am? Who is more believable than I am?*

So Paul traveled to many synagogues to share his newfound faith in Messiah Yeshua with his brethren the Jews. But when they rejected his teaching, the Lord spoke to Paul and said to him, *Paul, they're not going to believe your testimony. I'm sending you far away to the Gentiles.*

Paul then declared that he and Barnabas would "now turn to the Gentiles. For this is what the Lord has commanded us: 'I have made you a light for the Gentiles, that you may bring salvation to the ends of the earth'" (Acts 13:46–47).

Again, because the Jews would not believe, Paul was sent to the Gentiles. But look at the result: Their rejection of the Messiah has been the reconciliation of the world through the spread of the Gospel.

God is making of Abraham a "great nation" and blessing the world through him. There are no second-class citizens in the Kingdom of God. Jew and Gentile have become one in Messiah. If you are a Gentile believer in Yeshua, you have actually been grafted into the vine, and the supernatural blessings given to Abraham also flow out to you: "In Christ Jesus the blessing of Abraham [comes] to the Gentiles" (Galatians 3:13–14; see Romans 11:16–24). You have the full blessing of God on your life. You are now the "Israel of God" (Galatians 6:16).

End-Time Impartation

The latter part of Romans 11:15 tells us of the second stage of fulfillment of God's promise. If the Gentiles were blessed when the Jews did *not* believe (through the spread of the Gospel), how much more will they be blessed when the Jews *do* believe! Read this verse again: "If [the Jews'] rejection is the reconciliation of the world, what will their acceptance be but life from the dead?"

God has promised a supernatural end-time impartation as Jewish believers come to faith. In fact, when a critical mass of Jews like myself comes to faith in Jesus, this will usher in Jesus' return (see Romans 11:25–27). Zechariah 8:23 also speaks about this: "Thus says the LORD of hosts, 'In those days ten men from all the nations will grasp the garment of a Jew, saying, "Let us go with you, for we have heard that God is with you."'"

I come face-to-face with this even now as I travel to different parts of the world. Everywhere I go in Africa, for instance, the people are amazed that a Jewish believer is coming to them. I was in Gulu, Uganda, recently, which has been a place of tremendous bloodshed in the recent past. Now order has been restored. When I arrived, I was treated to incredible fanfare. I was escorted to the VIP entrance in the airport, and from there I was honored with a parade that extended about two miles and featured a military band. Thousands of people were holding banners and signs, welcoming me.

Some of the people told me that this event—God sending a Jewish believer to them—was so spectacular it could only mean that Jesus must be getting ready to come back. Their level of faith and their expectations were so high that thousands ran to the altar to get saved. Many supernatural signs and wonders took place, including the deaf hearing, the blind seeing, the lame walking and the demonized being delivered.

People in Africa and other places in the world recognize this dawning acceptance of the Gospel by the Jews as part of God's promised end-time impartation to the Church. And because they do, they receive a mighty anointing from Father God who spoke it. In this way God's blessing flows over the entire Church until He returns.

Now Is the Time

In these end-time days, the Church can be encouraged by God's faithfulness and move in the supernatural anointing that comes from association with the Jewish people. As the Lord has said to His people from ancient times, "I will bless those who bless you" (Genesis 12:3).

When you love what God loves, blessing comes upon you. It is a fact that the people you associate with impart to you what they are. This is why the person that you are going to be five years from now will be greatly influenced by the people you associate with, the books you read, the music you listen to, the entertainment you watch. When we put ourselves in alignment with the Jewish people in the correct way, some of the impartation on them, all the way back to Abraham, is transferred to us.

The Bible tells us this: "Pray for the peace of Jerusalem: 'May they prosper who love you'" (Psalm 122:6). Everyone who comes into agreement with God concerning His purposes for the Jews receives the anointing that flows through them. The supernatural blessing of God is poured out. The more our hearts are open and in alignment with God's heart, the greater the channel there is within us for God to pour forth into our lives.

I want to be in harmony with Him in every area of life so I can walk fully in His blessing and enter more and more into supernatural experience. And one of the decisions you and I must make in order to do this is to come into agreement with God's heart and thoughts regarding Israel and the Jewish people.

When your faith is placed in the supernatural God, the God of the ages who has revealed His power and presence in and through Israel, then you can begin to expect His supernatural presence in greater measure in your own life. It is one of the sure ways you can see the reality of God and His glory manifested physically on earth and come to expect signs and wonders. For most of us, this faith has room to grow. God *wants* it to grow. It begins with time in His presence, which is our next area of focus.

PART 2

Changing Your Expectations

4

Waiting on God

There is a term in Hebrew, *lees pog*, which means "to soak up." Soaking up involves waiting on the Lord. In our culture, this first step to experiencing the supernatural is sometimes our greatest challenge. We start to think, even in the pursuit of spiritual things, that if we *do* more, we can *become* more.

Before we can be productive, however, we first need to learn how to receive. We cannot give out that which we have not been given. And we receive best when we are resting in the Lord—when we are simply soaking in His presence without striving to do anything.

This concept is rooted in the Hebrew Bible and is a New Testament concept as well. First of all, we think of David— *David Melech Yisrael*, the king of Israel. It is no coincidence that the one individual Jesus is most closely linked to is David. At the end of the book of Revelation, for instance, Yeshua says, "I am the root and the offspring of David" (Revelation 22:16 KJV).

What did David know about this concept of simply resting in the Lord? In his beautiful and most famous psalm, David said, "The LORD is my shepherd, I shall not want. He makes me lie down in green pastures; He leads me beside quiet waters. He restores my soul" (Psalm 23:1–3). David's soul was being refreshed as the Lord led him to lie down and be still.

I had a dream that Cynthia and I were in an arena attending a rally. I noticed a battery charger on the ground next to where we were standing. We walked outside, and immediately Cynthia had something like a stroke. I was fearful and tried to wake her out of it. I realized that I needed the battery charger and ran to get it. It had a few holes in it, but it worked and she came to.

The Lord showed me that this was a dream about resting in Him. I was not recharging my "battery," and it was becoming unproductive. I was working all the time, rarely disconnecting from the world and resting in God. Plus, I was not giving Cynthia the time we needed together.

This is the same principle Yeshua described when He said, "The Sabbath was made for man" (Mark 2:27). The word *sabbath* means "to rest." God built into our lives this need for rest, and as we rest in Him, He restores us.

The Lord gave us this understanding when He created for six days and then rested on the seventh (see Genesis 2:1–2). We know that God does not become weary. Rather, as Jesus said, this principle is for us. This rest is a gift. It is built into creation. Notice also that this is not about law; God demonstrated the principle of rest before the Law was given. Without learning to rest and receive, we will not be able to move in the power of the Spirit or enter into a consistently supernatural walk with God.

Much of the time—probably most of the time—God is not asking us to do something for Him. He is asking us, rather, to sit and receive from Him. We think that by going about doing our "Christian things" or spiritual things, we are working for the Lord, but that is not ministry.

Ministry is a natural overflow from abiding in Yeshua and having His life pour forth from us. In this way, we fulfill the Lord's mandate: "You shall be My witnesses both in Jerusalem, and in all Judea and Samaria, and even to the remotest part of the earth" (Acts 1:8). In saying this Jesus did not necessarily mean that we need to fly all over the world. He was saying that *as we go where He calls us*, we will be His witnesses. Ministry is the natural overflow of having been in communion with and abiding in Him. When we have developed this intimacy with Jesus, people will be drawn to Him because of the reality of His presence in our lives. It will flow through us.

Again, this is a concept we need to learn and practice in order to get up and walk in the supernatural. Jesus said, "I am the vine, you are the branches; he who abides in Me and I in him, he bears much fruit, for apart from Me you can do nothing" (John 15:5). Any attempt to bear fruit begins at the place of abiding in Him.

I mentioned earlier that after my conversion I began to do every activity I could think of to get closer to God, but I achieved only burnout. I had not found what I was looking for, this place of intimacy, this sense of His abiding presence, and the outflowing experience of the supernatural. It was not until the Lord spoke to me and told me that the Kingdom of God is "within" that I was able to get in touch with the concept of soaking in His presence, asking Him to reveal Himself to me.

Once I made that transition to stop doing and start receiving, I experienced a new empowerment over my life regarding the supernatural. And the same will be true for every child of God who draws near to Him through the Holy Spirit. Something will happen. You will begin to receive revelation of His presence and demonstration of His power such as you never have before.

Receiving Him, All Day Long

"As many as *received* Him, to them He gave the right to become children of God, even to those who believe in His name" (John 1:12, emphasis added). Many people think that receiving Jesus is a one-time thing. This verse, however, speaks of more than the initial reception of Messiah into our lives. This is about receiving Him every day all day long. Think of it like your body's requirement for nourishing food. If you deprive your system of the proteins, vitamins and minerals that it needs to stay healthy, it will soon lose strength. Just so, without an ongoing refreshing from the presence of Yeshua, your spiritual walk runs the risk of becoming stagnant, weak and ineffective. As you learn to receive Him more and more and more through rest, you develop greater capacity to receive, and your greater capacity to receive means greater outflow of His presence through your life in supernatural experience and demonstration.

You remember Yeshua's visit with Mary and Martha, and how Martha was busy doing many things. And, true, can you think of a greater act of service than being able to serve Messiah Yeshua dinner in your home? What an awesome thing!

But we know the story. Mary was sitting at His feet and Martha became upset that she was not helping. What was Mary doing? She was receiving. That is all she was doing. She was not praying; she was not striving; she was not working. She was just sitting at His feet receiving.

Martha was frustrated because it looked to her as though Mary was being lazy. She said, "Yeshua, look at Mary. She's not helping."

And Yeshua said, "Martha, Martha. You are concerned about so many things, but Mary has chosen the one good necessary thing, the one good necessary part. And," Yeshua said, "it will never be taken away from her."

What does that mean? Yeshua was saying that sitting at His feet, receiving, is the first and most important thing. It is the one necessary thing. Yeshua is saying to you and me, "If you will learn how to sit at My feet, you won't have to strive, and you won't have to work. Everything that needs to get done will get done."

Application Steps

David said this in Psalm 27:4: "One thing I have asked from the LORD, that I shall seek: That I may dwell in the house of the LORD all the days of my life, to behold the beauty of the LORD and to meditate in His temple." When you think about this, what David's heart panted for was simply to be in God's presence, to receive from Him and behold Him. That is why he continued in verse 14 to say, "Wait for the LORD."

How does this soaking, this waiting on God happen? It starts with the disciplines of place and time.

Place

Most of us are familiar with the words of Psalm 46:10. The Lord Himself is speaking through the psalmist and He says, "Be still, and know that I am God" (KJV). This means being still, literally, before the Lord.

To do this you will need a comfortable room or specific place in your home or apartment that is your prayer chamber. I realize that God is everywhere, yet even Jesus Himself often went on top of a mountain to a specific place to be alone with God. This should be an area where you are free from the temptations that pull you away from Him.

The Bible says that the Lord is a rewarder of those who diligently seek Him. The simple act of setting apart a place where you can soak in Jesus' presence is an expression of faith. The Lord sees this. As you come into that place—just showing up to draw near to Him—you are fulfilling the Lord's call on your life: "Draw near to God and He will draw near to you" (James 4:8). You come with no agenda. No prayer list. That is not what this is about. There is a time for those things, but this is not that time. Simply come to the Lord and sit at His feet.

It is helpful to play beautiful worship music as you sit in His presence, music that ascends vertically to the Lord as opposed to music about Him. Play music that calms and soothes the soul. There is something supernatural that we receive from the Holy Spirit as we listen to sanctified worship music. This is why Revelation 5:8 shows 24 elders before the throne of God, each one having a harp. This is where we get the concept of angels with harps. Why harps? The harps represent music. You recall that David was a harpist. This is also why Elisha called for a harpist as he was looking for a word from the Lord, as we read in 2 Kings 3:12–15. When the harpist began to play, the hand of God came upon the prophet. The Lord uses music in a powerful way to communicate and impart Himself.

Oftentimes when I am sitting in the Lord's presence with worship music playing, it will birth within me a spirit of prayer. I am not forcing myself to pray. The Holy Spirit seems to use the music to begin to massage my soul and to loosen my ability to express myself to the Lord.

You can even see this concept being played out in the natural world. Think about some of the dramatic movies you have seen. When something significant begins to occur in the movie, it will be mixed with music in the background. Hollywood knows that music affects the soul in a mysterious way that no other vehicle can.

God is calling you. He is saying, "Just be still before Me and know that I am God. As you practice this discipline, I will pour My strength and peace into you."

Time

Once your place of prayer is ready, let me encourage you to set time apart every single day to be in His presence. And then commit to at least a half hour, though the longer the better. I do not want to be legalistic about this, but, as I am sure you would agree, in order for a relationship to grow, people must spend time together. The same rule applies in your relationship with God at an even higher level.

I had a dream once that I was in a room, a really simple room, with a table and two chairs. I was in one chair and a man was across from me in the other chair. I could not see his face, but I knew he was a friend.

I had been sitting there for hours, and I was growing bored and antsy. I wanted to get busy doing something. I was just about to do something to escape the feeling of being stuck in this room sitting across from the man when the Lord spoke to me.

He said, *This familiar friend that you have been sitting across from is Jesus. And if you will just stay put—stay seated, facing Him, waiting on Him—you will be made whole.*

It is worth pointing out that this was not easy to do in the dream, and neither is it easy to do in real life. It is a spiritual discipline, but, as we have noted, Paul points out that bodily discipline is profitable, but spiritual discipline is even more profitable.

Again, you do not have to force yourself to pray. Just sit and wait and trust. It is true that this takes discipline; trying it once to see if you like it will not cut it. Jesus gave the illustration of the sower going out to sow his seed. The seed that fell on shallow, rocky soil built no root system and did not last long. But the seed that fell on good, deep soil put down roots and bore fruit (see Mark 4:3–20).

I hope you are coming to understand how important it is to take the time to receive from God. Many of us need to come out of the lifestyles we have been leading. We are busy all the time, and then we run to church or a Messianic synagogue and think somehow that is adequate.

It really is not adequate.

If we want to saturate our lives with God's presence—if we want to meet Him and know Him and touch Him so that He becomes more real to us than anything else in life—it is going to take time with God every day.

Yeshua says, "Come to Me, all who are weary and heavy-laden, and I will give you rest." We need to turn back to the ancient Hebrew practice of simply sitting at the Lord's feet. There remains a Sabbath rest, Scripture says, for the people of God.

A Source of Strength

In the midst of Scripture we find a verse that is full of reve-lation and insight that many have overlooked: "In quietness and trust is your strength" (Isaiah 30:15). During your quiet time you may want to pray something like this:

Father, I come to You. Your Holy Spirit is real. Your Ruach HaKodesh *is real. I pray that You will give me revelation concerning Your presence around me. Let me understand how close You are to me.*

Father, I come to You. Will You bring me to the reali-zation that Your Spirit is inside me? Will You confirm to me my identity as Your child? Let me know who I am in You, Lord. Let me know how much You love me.

Father, I come to You, waiting on You. I am asking You to enlarge my soul and my capacity to receive You. Increase my ability to sense Your Spirit. Strengthen me with Your truth. I am asking You to empower me. I am asking You to impart more of Jesus to me. Let me see in a greater way how much You are working in my life. Let me begin to move in supernatural authority.

Remember as you develop the discipline of waiting that this is not a quick fix. This is not a magic pill. This is quiet awareness of truth and reality that brings peace and super-natural power. As you come near to Him and sit before Him, He promises that over time you will sense a growing reve-lation of His love. He will be making His abode with you, quietly reframing the habitation where He dwells.

God's purpose is to reveal Himself to you in an intimate and personal way through the *Ruach HaKodesh*. As you come out from the world and spend time sitting before Him, Yeshua promises, "I will make My home with you. You will be loved by My Father, and I will love you."

This is the passion of my heart and I pray it is yours—that Jesus promises to be more real to you and me than anything else in life. When that is true, then it does not matter where you go, where you live, where you are. The thing that you are going to be most conscious of in your life is the presence of Jesus Himself.

This experience of waiting on God is key for laying a foundation from which the supernatural will become natural in your life. Make a commitment to spend time every day sitting before Him, soaking at His feet. Play beautiful spiritual music. As you do this, believe that He is going to come to you. He is going to manifest Himself to you.

Trust in the process. Do not look just for the spectacular, but be confident that over time you are being supernaturally charged and changed even if you cannot tell that something is happening. I promise you that if you will be faithful to this practice unto the Lord, things are going to change in your life. And you are going to fall in love with Him and know Him in a greater way than ever before. Trust me. Be patient. And stick to this plan. A parent might not see growth in a child each day because of the ongoing contact, but a relative who comes for visits notices the changes. It is the same for you. You might not be able to detect the growth in yourself, but I can assure you from personal experience that you are going to be changed if you will stick to this process—not out of legalism, but out of your love for the Lord and desire for more of His supernatural presence in your life.

Waiting on God and sensing His presence is its own reward, but there are many other benefits as well. In that place of quiet, where His voice is clearest, your discernment grows. The process we might call divine intuition—where you have an inner knowing about something—begins to take shape.

This takes practice. In the next chapter you will learn to recognize how the Spirit speaks to you through words and images. And as you learn to hear the Spirit's voice more clearly, you will be able to move forward with greater confidence and receive specific guidance from the Lord in your life.

5

Becoming Spirit-Conscious

God does not speak most often in the earthquake or roaring fire. He usually does not speak in the violent or the spectacular or the dramatic. Rather, He speaks most often in a still, small voice with words, pictures and impressions. These ways that the Father communicates are so subtle that if we are not paying attention, we will miss them.

Jesus said, "He who has an ear, let him hear what the Spirit says" (Revelation 2:29)—the point being that the Spirit is speaking but not all are hearing. This is true for both the Church as a corporate body and also us as individuals.

Let me give you an example. Years ago I was teaching a Bible study in a church building on a Saturday morning. In the middle of the study a man whom I had never met walked into the room. As soon as I saw him, I felt strongly impressed to stand up, walk over to him and blow my shofar over him. But that impression seemed so bizarre and out of the box to me that I did not act on it.

As the man drew closer, I said, "Can I help you?"

And he said, "I am here to buy a shofar."

That incident jarred me because I realized that I need to pay close attention to the voice of the Holy Spirit in my life.

One time recently I was contemplating whether or not I should move forward with a particular decision. As I was sitting there thinking about it, an image flashed through my mind. It was a picture of a ball-and-socket joint, like a knee. One rounded bone was moving easily within a corresponding cup-shaped bone. They fit perfectly.

This picture was far out of my normal thinking process. I am not a doctor, I do not read about those types of things, and I had not been looking at that type of material. The thought did not originate with me; the Lord had given it. And when I caught the significance of His showing me a picture, I realized what He was telling me.

Yes, He was saying, *this decision is right for you to make. It fits your life right now. It's like a hand in a glove.*

If I had not paid attention to the wisp of a picture that went in and out of my thoughts, if I had ignored it because it was not overwhelming, then I would have missed it—and missed the direction I was praying to receive.

I can guarantee that if you are walking with God, you, too, have experienced these types of supernatural occurrences. It is possible, however, that you never knew the Lord was speaking to you because you did not recognize it as the voice of the Holy Spirit. Think of a time in your life when you sensed intuitively that the Spirit was leading you to do something or not do something, to say something or not say something. Did you catch it? Did you follow it?

You can grow in the skill of listening as one who is Spirit-conscious. The Holy Spirit is moving in your life, communicating Jesus' purposes to you. Jesus said that the Holy Spirit "will take of Mine and will disclose it to you" (John 16:14). This activity and movement is the way the Bible presents Him from the very beginning.

God's sacred name, *Yahweh*, is in fact a verb. It implies continuous, unfinished action. Knowing that the Spirit of the Lord is always moving, that He is speaking and acting in the present can lift you to a place of becoming more expectant to receive something from Him. He is the God of the now.

Application Steps

You and I were created in God's image and in His likeness. God, in essence, is Spirit. The first man and woman were created as spirit beings and communicated with God at a spirit level. But we know what happened. Adam and Eve lost spiritual connectivity with God. They fell and became body-conscious. They were already naked, but that had not been their focal point. They had been Spirit-conscious, but as soon as they fell, they became flesh-conscious.

Now it is our task to become Spirit-conscious once again. How does this work? How can we grow in being led by God's Spirit? Here is a strategy of five application steps that, in conjunction with the prayer room, will allow you to go higher in the supernatural experience of being able to discern His voice and be led by His Spirit.

Step One: Become Self-Aware

Let me ask you a question. Why do you look in a mirror? Is it because you want to see what you look like to the outer world?

There is nothing wrong, obviously, with taking care of ourselves and making sure we are presenting ourselves in an appropriate way. But the problem is that many of us are too focused on how we are coming across to everybody else. We look at ourselves from the outside in, rather than viewing things from the inside out.

I catch myself doing this. I notice sometimes in my thought life that I am not living life from within. Have you ever worried about what someone else is thinking? This kind of focus can erode a lot of the pleasure in life. Plus it is pointless. First of all, we probably have no idea what another person is thinking, and, second of all, it really does not matter.

If we are going to become Spirit-conscious and tune in to the Spirit's voice, we need to see life from the inside out. Another way to describe this is to become self-aware or to pay attention to the inner witness of our hearts. If we are going to discern the quiet voice of the Spirit, it is vital that we become more aware of what is going on inside us as opposed to being more connected to the outer world. As this happens, God is able to raise our supernatural awareness.

When I began to practice the discipline of waiting on God in the prayer room, the Lord led me into an even deeper place of silence before Him. It probably lasted a year or more. Whenever I had the opportunity, such as when I was driving or had free time at home, I did not turn to anything external—no music, no phone, no conversations, no television. I was just silent before the Lord. This period of silence was an important season in my life because it helped me become more conscious of my inner nature—what I was feeling, what I was thinking. It helped me develop my ability to sense intuitively what was going on inside of me and learn how to hear what the Holy Spirit was saying. I love Proverbs

20:27. It says that a person's spirit is the lamp of the Lord. In other words, where is God illuminating us from? From our spirits within.

As you are becoming more self-aware, it is also important to take time to grow in knowledge of the Word. This will keep you on track and prevent you from being deceived, because the Spirit and the Word are one. God will often speak through Scripture. He might "highlight" a particular passage while you are reading, impressing upon you that it applies to your particular situation. Or He might bring a verse to mind later when you need it.

Step Two: Act on What You Hear

"The anointing which you received from Him," John tells us, "abides in you, and you have no need for anyone to teach you; but as His anointing teaches you about all things, and is true and is not a lie, and just as it has taught you, you abide in Him" (1 John 2:27).

In Old Testament times anyone who needed a word from the Lord had to go to a prophet who could speak for God. Today, every believer has received an anointing from the Holy One. The Spirit of God is always with us, teaching us, training us, leading us, guiding us. We need only to affirm that truth.

Notice that John states pointedly that God's anointing "is not a lie." Why am I stressing this? Because many times the Holy Spirit has communicated to us through His anointing upon us, and yet we have not believed the word He was speaking.

Let me give you an example. There was a convenience mart located about a mile from where I once lived. I used to stop by there all the time and then continue on to work. On one particular day I picked up the items I needed and got back into my car. At that point I felt a clear impression of the Holy Spirit saying, *Don't go the usual way today. Don't go that way.*

This made no sense to me. So I said, "I think this is You, Lord. I'm even going so far as to declare that I think You just spoke to me about this. But because I have a little question about it, and it doesn't make sense to me, I'm going to go the way I usually go anyway. And if something goes wrong, I'll know that I heard Your Spirit speak to me. And I'll learn from this that I really do hear Your voice."

Sure enough, something went wrong. There was an accident in front of me and I was delayed in traffic. It wrecked my schedule. I had received a supernatural word from the Holy Spirit and ignored it. I should have recognized the anointing and thought, *That is not a lie.*

Consider Paul's example when he was trying to find a route to take the Gospel. When he was in a city called Troas, the Holy Spirit spoke to him:

> A vision appeared to Paul in the night: a man of Macedonia was standing and appealing to him, and saying, "Come over to Macedonia and help us." When he had seen the vision, immediately we sought to go into Macedonia, concluding that God had called us to preach the gospel to them.
>
> Acts 16:9–10

Paul trusted that this was the Lord speaking to him and followed the Spirit's leading.

Another way we act on what we hear is to follow the confirming witness of God's peace. I mentioned earlier that Revelation describes a sea of glass before the throne, which represents perfect peace and stillness. Romans 16:20 says that the God of peace will soon crush Satan under your feet. To be led by the Holy Spirit, we must be able to discern the peace of God.

If you are looking for direction, try to sense whether or not you have peace about saying something or taking a certain action. You can feel it. If you do not have peace about something, or if you actually feel a hesitation or "check" in your spirit, wait before moving forward. Abiding in God's peace is a sure way to be fruitful and to see supernatural results from your actions. Let God's process of sanctification do its full work.

If you feel God's peace and your heart bears witness to what you sense, go ahead and believe it and be willing to act on it. Supernatural events will not take place any other way.

Step Three: Realize That Your Senses Are Being Trained

As you practice these steps, then according to Hebrews 5:14, your senses will be trained. This means that you will be able to discern His voice more and more. There is no doubt that this process of growing in Spirit-consciousness can be scary. We all question our own discernment and look for corroboration. Sometimes we have a clear sense that we are hearing God, but other times we are not sure. If your heart is right and if you are stepping out in trust, God will train your senses. Over time you will learn to discern which impressions are from God and which are not.

Here is the beautiful thing: If you ask Jesus to sensitize your ears, He will. Then when God gives you illumination and you act on it, more is given and you enter into God's power and presence more and more.

Step Four: Let Go of the Pressure to Perform

All of us have felt pressure to perform—from ourselves and other people. I remember being in a church one time and standing in line to receive prayer. The ministry person put his hands on my shoulders and prayed for me. Then he pushed me. He tried to push me down as if I were falling under the power of the Spirit. I did not feel anything of a spiritual nature in this experience, and I was not going to fall down because it was part of his agenda. He finally stopped pushing me and moved to the next person in line.

I do not know that prayer minister's motive. Was it to look good? Was it a need to perform on his part? Was it a belief that I would be better off for it?

One thing I do know: There is no satisfaction in faking a supernatural experience. God comes on people at times, but we cannot control—nor do we have to control—where and when He comes. Sometimes I know that someone is going to be healed, but I have no idea who it is. And I am relaxed about this because I know that I cannot heal anybody and it is up to God. The point is, if we are gong to experience the authentic supernatural presence of the Holy Spirit, we cannot give in to the pressure to try to make it happen.

It is important when moving in the supernatural not to let it be a burden or a place of anxiety or fear. You do not have to prove to anyone who you are. In fact, walking in the supernatural begins with knowing who you already are. Before Jesus did any miracle, He knew who He was. His identity had been confirmed by the Father's voice: "You are My beloved Son, in whom I am well-pleased."

Being Spirit-conscious means doing your best to remain at peace. You step out as you are led, and your faith leads to experience. I like to think of the fire and cloud over the Tabernacle (see Numbers 9:15–22). Whenever it stayed in place, the Israelites stayed in place. Whenever it moved, they moved. Whenever it stopped, they stopped. I want to encourage you to look at God's leading like this instead of being driven by nervousness, fear or ambition. Follow the witness of the Holy Spirit.

Quite frankly, the Lord can do something supernatural in us or through us at any time—sometimes when we least expect it; oftentimes when we do not deserve it. Anybody can experience a miracle: Balaam's donkey talked to him. To walk in the supernatural consistently, however, we must cooperate with the spiritual principles of the Kingdom.

The Holy Spirit is on earth right now, revealing the Father to you and revealing the Son to you. If you are not looking for Him, if you have not trained your spiritual senses to recognize Him, then He can be knocking on the door of your heart all day long, but you will never know it.

Perhaps you would like to confess this to God right now.

Father, forgive me for allowing myself to be driven by forces other than You. I am a willing vessel. I am not going to bow down to the pressure to perform. I don't have to prove anything. I'm going to abide in Your peace and do my best to remain in You.

Step Five: Beware a Seared Conscience

I want to mention something further about the importance of repentance in the context of being Spirit-conscious. If we know we are missing the mark and are walking in rebellion, and we continue to reject His guidance or leading, the rebellion can spread in our hearts like poison. There is a balance between recognizing the love of God and understanding the fear of God. If we knowingly refuse the Holy Spirit's illumination of sin in our lives, we are putting ourselves in danger. Consider God's words in 2 Thessalonians 2:8–12:

> That lawless one will be revealed whom the Lord will slay with the breath of His mouth and bring to an end by the appearance of His coming; that is, the one whose coming is in accord with the activity of Satan, with all power and signs and false wonders, and with all the deception of wickedness for those who perish, because they did not receive the love of the truth so as to be saved. For this reason God will send upon them a deluding influence so that they will believe what is false, in order that they all may be judged who did not believe the truth, but took pleasure in wickedness.

God is saying here that those who close off their hearts to the love of God seal their own doom. As a result of the rejection of truth, God actually "will send upon them a deluding influence so that they will believe what is false."

Keep in mind that this word was not written to those who want to draw near to God but to those who have confirmed in their own hearts their decision to walk away from Him. It is, however, a stark warning. When the Holy Spirit nudges us about sin, we will either affirm His truth or strike back in self-defense. If we refuse to affirm what the Lord is saying, we will make excuses and blame others.

If we continue in this deception, Scripture says that our consciences can become seared. It follows that the Holy Spirit may withdraw from us. If that happens, we lose the ability to be led by the Spirit. We will no longer be Spirit-conscious. This is very serious. The Bible says that God will not strive with us forever. That is why Jesus said to the church in Ephesus, "If you don't repent, if you don't turn to Me, if you don't bring yourself into alignment with My Spirit in your life, I'm going to remove My presence from you" (see Revelation 2:5).

The Holy Spirit is the one illuminating our consciences; the New Testament describes pure religion as having a pure conscience before God (see 2 Timothy 1:3). Paul wrote further of this relationship between his conscience and the Holy Spirit: "I am telling the truth in Christ, I am not lying, my conscience testifies with me in the Holy Spirit" (Romans 9:1).

He also wrote, "[Keep] faith and a good conscience, which some have rejected and suffered shipwreck in regard to their faith" (1 Timothy 1:19). If the Holy Spirit has been convicting you in any area of your life and you have an ongoing guilty conscience, that is rebellion. It is unwillingness to yield to what you know the Spirit is telling you. From there it is possible to spiral downward into shipwreck. This is why rebellion is such a dangerous position—because it can cause you to break fellowship with God.

If, however, you are eager to hear His voice, you can be sure that the Holy Spirit is gracious when you miss it. If you are sincerely trying but are going the wrong direction, He will help you discover that you are knocking your head against a wall. He will help you pick up and move on, having learned a valuable lesson.

Jesus spoke to the woman at the well and said, "An hour is coming, and now is, when the true worshipers will worship the Father in spirit and truth; for such people the Father seeks to be His worshipers. God is spirit" (John 4:23–24).

In other words, the Father is looking for those who long for intimate communion with Him. As you

- become self-aware,
- act on what you hear,
- realize that your senses are being trained,
- let go of the pressure to perform, and
- beware a seared conscience,

you will develop inner, intuitive awareness. The Spirit of God is faithful to make His voice known in your life. He is bearing witness with your spirit all day long, every single day. Walk in confidence, knowing that His Spirit is guiding you. He will lead you from one supernatural realm to another.

6

What Are Signs, Wonders and Miracles?

Much of the Church in the Western world fails to understand that Christianity is rooted in and operates in the supernatural. Unfortunately, teaching persists that signs, wonders and miracles ceased when the apostles died or when the canon of Scripture was completed. A large part of the Church reads about what God did for other people without realizing that Jesus is the same yesterday, today and forever.

Even from the very beginning we see in the Torah that our faith is rooted in the supernatural. Consider it: God floods the earth and saves Noah through a supernatural word of revelation. He parts the Red Sea. He parts the Jordan River. He causes the sun to stand still for Joshua and his troops.

Jesus appears on the scene. He opens blind eyes. He walks on water. He raises the dead. He ascends up into the sky as His followers watch Him disappear into the clouds.

Then the disciples go to Jerusalem, and after fifty days the Spirit of the living God, of *Elohim* Himself, appears visibly above them. They begin to speak supernaturally in languages they do not know. The journey continues with Peter, James, John and the other disciples, who do miracles everywhere they go.

We could go on and on and on. The point is, whenever the Gospel is preached, we should expect it to be confirmed with signs, wonders and miracles so that, as Paul explained, people's faith would rest not in "persuasive words of wisdom but in demonstration of the Spirit and of power" (1 Corinthians 2:4). Just recently I prayed for a fifteen-year-old boy who had never been able to hear or speak. His twenty-year-old sister was with him, and when God healed him, she was amazed.

"This is the first time that he has ever spoken in his entire life," she said. "I saw these things on television, but I didn't know if they were real. Now I've seen them for myself."

We can—and should—look for the supernatural in our lives. I believe that we can go farther than Paul or Peter or John. Why not? Jesus said that all things are possible to him who believes. Why should there be a lid on it? I have seen people being healed supernaturally of all types of things. And consider the ministry of Reinhard Bonnke, who has led millions of people in Africa to the Lord.

It relates to expectant faith. I was ministering in Uganda recently, preaching and teaching to a large crowd for about four days. There was one man who sat in the front row in the same place every night. His eyes were wide open and stayed locked on me the entire time he sat there. He was being saturated with the Word; he was receiving it like a sponge. And as I was preaching, I thought, *I want to be a source of blessing to this man. I believe this man is expecting to receive.*

So I asked someone to bring him to me and I began to prophesy over him. I told him that he was about to receive something. I had full faith that he was about to be given a dramatic and powerful impartation of the Spirit of the Lord. I laid my hands on him and it was as though a wrecking ball had swung through the air and hit him in the chest. He was a big guy; it took two other men to hold him up. Tears began to roll down his face. That man received a powerful infilling of the Holy Spirit because he believed, and he was fully expecting Jesus to act.

Special Acts of God

Signs, wonders and miracles are special acts of God that signify His supernatural intervention in the natural. These might be things like healing and deliverance—supernatural phenomena that we can see, feel or experience. The main thing is that the occurrences are so unusual we know beyond doubt they are not of this world. They are happening not in an ordinary way but in a "super" ordinary way. They prove God's presence in our lives and the lives of those around us.

Although some people teach that signs, wonders and miracles are all distinct and separate from each other, I have found that they are often interrelated. We cannot neatly separate the three. There are, however, a few general distinctions.

Signs

The Hebrew word for *sign* is *oth*. A sign is designed to get your attention. Like a wonder and a miracle, a sign is a manifestation that points to the reality of God. Signs are generally discerned with your intellect; a sign is not a sign if you cannot detect it in the natural world. God breaks into your circumstances and does something to get your attention in order to warn you or lead you on the right path. Sometimes God uses signs simply to help you know that He is real and present with you.

I read recently the story of Loren Cunningham, founder of Youth With A Mission, who wanted to purchase a ship to be used in ministry, but he had no money, resources or staff for such a vision. Still, he called his team together to pray about this, even though in the natural it seemed impossible. As they prayed, they heard a knock at the door. It was a man, whom Loren had never met. The man said basically, "I know this sounds strange, but I feel called to be a missionary even though I feel unqualified to be a missionary. All I have ever known is the sea. I am a seaman." That experience was so astounding to the team, they knew God had given them a sign to pursue their vision for ministry.

I remember a time in my own life when I set out from my home to drive with my evangelistic team to a church north of Cleveland, where we would minister. After about two and a half hours, we decided to stop in Cleveland to get a bite to eat in a Jewish delicatessen there. Just as we were opening the door to walk in, my father walked out. What was the chance of my driving two and a half hours into Cleveland, and my dad, who lives in Cleveland and who was unaware that I was coming, walking out of the restaurant at the exact same time that I was walking in? To me that was a sign that God was up to something, which I pointed out to my dad. I said, "Dad, Jesus wants to get your attention!"

I try to point these types of things out to people when they are in the midst of experiencing something that in the natural they might assume to be a coincidence. Often, when you have eyes to see, you know it is the supernatural. Just recently I was dealing with a very difficult situation over the phone. Talking with that person really took a lot out of me. He continued to mess up a particular situation he was involved in.

The next day I got a text from a friend. He wrote, "I had a dream last night that you were on the phone with someone and became frustrated. I don't ordinarily dream about you, so I felt it was significant."

I knew instantly that the Lord was letting me know that He loves me, that He understood, that He was with me, and to be at peace. Since that time God opened a door for me to be freed from the situation with the individual that was so frustrating and challenging.

Scripture is full of God speaking through signs. The most well known are probably the signs Moses demonstrated to Pharaoh and his court of magicians. God directed Moses to throw his staff on the ground, and it turned into a serpent. "If they will not believe you or heed the witness of the first sign," God said, "they may believe the witness of the last sign" (Exodus 4:8).

Gideon asked God for a sign: "Gideon said to Him, 'If now I have found favor in Your sight, then show me a sign that it is You who speak with me'" (Judges 6:17). How many of us have had that experience? We have an intuitive sense that the Spirit of the Lord is communicating something to us or leading us a certain way. We think it is God, we kind of know it is God, but we need a little confirmation. And so we say, "If this is You, Lord, show me a sign."

That is what was happening here. The Lord was literally standing in front of Gideon as an angel, and Gideon said, "If this is really You, God, I mean, I think it's You, but if it's really You, I'm going to go prepare an offering, and I'm asking You still to be here when I get back." And the Lord supernaturally gave Gideon that sign.

In fact, Jesus' first miracle was when He turned the water to wine. And the Scripture says this was the first of many signs that Jesus did. Signs were very much a part of Jesus' ministry. That is why John wrote, "This beginning of His signs Jesus did in Cana of Galilee, and manifested His glory, and His disciples believed in Him" (John 2:11).

Jesus even gave His disciples signs regarding His return. "The disciples asked Him, 'What will be the sign of the coming of the end of the age and of Your return?'" (Matthew 24:3). They wanted to know how to discern when this age is going to end—what will be the sign of it? Jesus gave them many examples—earthquakes, famines, wars, sickness, pestilence, rumors of wars, people's love growing cold, false prophets, false teachers, and on and on—all signs.

Although our faith does not rest first and foremost in signs, but rather in the Word, signs are not to be ignored. Maybe, for instance, you are seeking God's will in your life, and God is telling you that the direction you are headed is not correct. You should not ignore those signs, because if you keep pushing at the wrong door, you could end up suffering a lot of needless pain and frustration.

I remember back in the 1980s when I was starting a church. Cynthia and I were looking for a place to live. Someone approached me and said, "I just bought a house, and I would like to invite you and your wife to live in the house with me. I don't need all this room." It was a generous invitation, but because I did not know the person, I chose to follow my own comfort level and live someplace else—which ended up being a very uncomfortable and difficult living arrangement. If I had heeded the sign of this man coming to me and offering us his house to live in, I believe in retrospect that my wife and I would have been much more at peace in that situation.

My point is, although our faith does not rest solely in signs, neither should we ignore them. God wants to have our attention, and sometimes He does it by manifesting Himself supernaturally in the physical world through signs.

Wonders

Wonder comes from the Hebrew word *mopheth*. A wonder shocks. It takes your breath away. Signs and wonders intersected as God led the children of Israel out of Egypt: "You brought Your people Israel out of the land of Egypt with signs and with wonders, and with a strong hand and with an outstretched arm and with great terror" (Jeremiah 32:21). Psalm 135:9 affirms, "He sent signs and wonders into your midst, O Egypt." Psalm 106:21–22 says, "God their Savior [did] great things in Egypt, wonders in the land of Ham and awesome things by the Red Sea."

Speaking of Moses, Scripture says, "Since that time no prophet has risen in Israel like Moses, whom the LORD knew face to face, for all the signs and wonders which the LORD sent him to perform in the land of Egypt against Pharaoh, all his servants, and all his land" (Deuteronomy 34:10–11).

Notice in the New Testament that Peter's healing of the lame man was a wonder: "With a leap he stood upright and he began to walk; and he entered the temple with them, walking and leaping and praising God. And all the people saw him walking and praising God . . . and they were filled with wonder and amazement at what had happened to him" (Acts 3:8–10). The God we worship manifested Himself throughout biblical history with wonders, and He is still doing the same today.

Sometimes God manifests Himself with a spiritual wonder through dramatically delivering someone of a demon. This can be so shocking that those who witness it are left speechless as God manifests His glory. An experience of this type of wonder happened one time in Gulu, Uganda, as we ministered to thousands of people in the name of Jesus. It was so otherworldly and beyond control I did not know where it was going. It was much bigger than anything I had ever seen, as hundreds of people began to manifest demons and get set free at the same time. It almost felt as though pandemonium was about to explode. Many souls were saved that day as God revealed His supernatural power through that wonder.

Miracles

The most common Hebrew word for *miracle* is *pala*. This is a divine occurrence that supersedes natural law. The most noteworthy example is the resurrection of Jesus. A miracle can also be both a sign and a wonder. It is interesting that Jesus' first miracle, turning water into wine, was a miracle of joy. Wine in Scripture is a symbol of joy. Our God is a happy God. He wants us to experience His supernatural presence. As I indicated, signs, wonders and miracles are not always separate but are oftentimes interconnected.

Let me give you a personal example. Several years ago I dreamed that I was walking along with a friend of mine from high school. This friend had been a tremendous athlete as a student. I had excelled at wrestling but was not an all-around athlete, excelling in every sport like he did.

In the dream, I was accompanying my friend on his way to try out for a baseball team. When we got to the field, we approached the coach. But rather than look at my friend, the coach turned to face me. This surprised me because I was not trying out for the team.

Then the coach said, "I am going to be watching you very closely from this point forward. Everything you have done in the past is washed under the bridge. What you do now will determine whether or not I put you in the majors."

I awoke and felt that this was a "God dream." I wrote it in my journal but forgot about it until I came across it a few years later.

When I saw the dream in my journal, I was filled with dread—not because I doubted my salvation, but because I realized that with God watching my every move, impulse, thought, feeling, there was not even the slightest chance I would make it to the "majors." I was not doing anything immoral, but I knew all too well the ongoing struggle every human has to battle the flesh and renew the mind.

Now I do not recommend doing what I did next, by the way, but because I had no hope, I decided I might as well face the sad truth and let the hammer come down on my head. So I prayed a defeated prayer, saying that I was going to open my Bible and put my finger on a word. I asked God to let that word be my answer as to whether or not I had made it into the "majors"—and I felt sure the word my finger was going to land on would be something about failure, revealing my stumbling too many times in my attempts to fight the good fight of faith.

I closed my eyes, opened my Bible and put my finger on the page. When I looked down, I could not believe what I was seeing. My finger was pointing to the word *major*. I was stunned. I had no idea the word *major* was even in the Bible! It was as though a prophecy from Isaiah had just crashed into my world: "See and recognize . . . that the hand of the Lord has done this" (Isaiah 41:20).

I went to a concordance and discovered that out of an estimated 800,000 words in the Bible, the word *major* appears *one time.* My "chance" of pointing to that word on my own was 1 in 800,000—in other words, supernatural. This was the act of a gracious and merciful God smiling down His encouragement on one of His children. It was a sign that got my attention, a wonder that took my breath away—and a miracle because it superseded the natural order of things!

Should We Seek for Signs?

So let me ask you a question for consideration. What should our position be regarding signs? Should we ask for them? Should we be afraid of them? Should we take the position that it is dangerous to look for them? We do not want to focus on signs, but, unfortunately, I think the reverse has been true. A lot of teaching on this subject is negative. We are taught that looking for the supernatural is dangerous and a bad thing. We miss the fact that the written Word of God includes signs, wonders and miracles as very much a part of the biblical history of the life of God's people. My position is that we should not only believe in them but be sensitive to them, and expect them.

Look at the story of King Ahaz told in Isaiah 7. God told the king through the prophet Isaiah to ask for a sign regarding a particular military outcome. The Lord said to Ahaz, "Ask a sign for yourself from the LORD your God; make it as deep as Sheol or high as heaven" (verse 11).

Now notice Ahaz' response: "I will not ask, nor will I test the LORD!" (verse 12).

You know what? God was angry with him for saying that! Isaiah responded to the king, "Is it too slight a thing for you to try the patience of men, that you will try the patience of my God as well? Therefore the Lord Himself will give you a sign: Behold, a virgin will be with child and bear a son, and she will call His name Immanuel" (verses 13–14). Sometimes God wants to reveal Himself through a miraculous confirmation.

In 2 Kings 20 we read about another king's failure regarding a sign. King Hezekiah had a mortal illness—he was going to die. In his grief he prayed to the Lord, and God heard his prayer. The Lord spoke to him through Isaiah and said, "I will add fifteen years to your life, and I will deliver you . . . from the hand of the king of Assyria" (verse 6).

Hezekiah was not completely sure he was healed, so he asked for a sign. He said, "What will be the sign that the LORD will heal me, and that I shall go up to the house of the LORD the third day?" (verse 8).

Isaiah responded by asking the king which sign he would prefer: Did he want a shadow on the stairway to go forward ten steps or backward ten steps?

Hezekiah answered, "It is easy for the shadow to decline ten steps; no, but let the shadow turn backward ten steps" (verse 10). In other words, the shadow went back up the ten steps it had just gone down. Some people describe it as the sun going backward. What a sign!

Although this miraculous sign was given, notice how Hezekiah responded: He did not believe it. Here is what Scripture records about it: "He prayed to the LORD, and the LORD spoke to him and gave him a sign. But Hezekiah gave no return for the benefit he received, because his heart was proud;

therefore wrath came on him and on Judah and Jerusalem"
(2 Chronicles 32:24–25).

Hezekiah failed to heed the sign God gave him; he did not
pay attention; he did not receive it; it did not change him.
And the wrath of God fell on Judah and Jerusalem because
of it. When the Bible speaks of the wrath of God, such as
in this instance, I think it is not about hatred or anger but
about judgment and discipline. Judgment and discipline can
be hard. In this instance they were necessary because Hezekiah's heart was proud.

How many of us have been guilty of asking the Lord for a
sign, which He gives, but then we are not impressed enough
to let it change us? We give it no return. I am ashamed to
admit that many times I have asked the Lord for a sign, and
He has given me one, but instead of being fully convinced,
I ask Him for another one. Thank God for His mercy and
longsuffering!

We should not live by signs to the extent that we need
a new sign every five minutes to feel secure in God. If our
approach is, "Lord, give me a sign! Lord, give me another
sign! Lord, show me one more time and I'll believe You,"
that is obviously not going to lead us down the road of life.
But neither do we deny their reality and *not* look for them.
We need balance.

Authentication of Ministry

Those whom Jesus ministered to while He was on earth in
the flesh did not have leather-bound Bibles with 66 books
that they carried around and had in their homes. Most people
did not get saved by doing a Scripture study; most people
got saved when the Gospel was preached, followed by signs,

wonders and miracles. John 20:30–31 explains this: "Therefore many other signs Jesus also performed in the presence of the disciples, which are not written in this book, but these have been written so that you may believe that Jesus is the Christ, the Son of God; and that believing you may have life in His name."

When Jesus took five loaves and two fish and fed five thousand people miraculously, they called it a sign. And when they saw the sign, they believed (see John 6:14).

When Philip preached the Gospel in Samaria, "The crowds with one accord were giving attention to what was said by Philip, as they heard and saw the signs which he was performing" (Acts 8:5–6).

As soon as the Holy Spirit came at Pentecost, signs spread like wildfire. The Scripture says this: "Everyone kept feeling a sense of awe; and many wonders and signs were taking place" (Acts 2:43).

Peter and John prayed, "Grant that Your bond-servants may speak Your word with all confidence, while You extend Your hand to heal, and signs and wonders take place through the name of Your holy servant Jesus" (Acts 4:29–30).

Paul appealed to signs and wonders to authenticate his ministry: "For I will not presume to speak of anything except what Christ has accomplished through me, resulting in the obedience of the Gentiles by word and deed, in the power of signs and wonders, in the power of the Spirit" (Romans 15:18–19).

Who can deny this phenomenon of God confirming the Gospel with signs and wonders? Why would anyone want to? Why would anyone not want to believe in a God who is as present and active today as He was in the early Church? He is. Jesus is the same yesterday, today and forever. Scripture is clear about this; it would take willful opposition to the supernatural dimension of God's activity in the world in order not to believe it. Our God is a supernatural God, and because He is supernatural, we should expect the supernatural in our lives today. To reject this is to resist the plain truth of God's Word and rely on man-made tradition.

As I have mentioned, many people have been taught that these miracle gifts ceased when the apostles died or when the Bible was fully written. There is absolutely no scriptural basis for such a position. None. Why would Paul say that gifts of the Spirit include gifts of healing and miracles as well as many other supernatural gifts if they did not exist in the Church today (see 1 Corinthians 12:9–10)? These verses were written for every generation of believers.

God still backs up His Word so that His Word might be believed. Because the Holy Spirit is here, we should not expect anything less than the types of phenomena we see happening in the New Testament. God is a supernatural God, and He builds His Kingdom supernaturally.

> How will we escape if we neglect so great a salvation? After it was at the first spoken through the Lord, it was confirmed to us by those who heard, God also testifying with them, both by signs and wonders and by various miracles and by gifts of the Holy Spirit according to His own will.
>
> Hebrews 2:3–4

Jesus gave us this charge: "These signs will accompany those who have believed: in My name they will cast out demons, they will speak with new tongues; . . . they will lay hands on the sick, and they will recover" (Mark 16:17–18). If we do not have a supernatural ministry, we are not living in the fullness of our callings. We need to be out there teaching Jesus, proclaiming Jesus, inviting people to Jesus, laying our hands on people, praying for them, cursing devils, declaring prophetic words over people's lives. When we step out in faith and share the Gospel, God is going to work with us and confirm His Word with signs and wonders.

Only Believe!

Signs, wonders and miracles, especially those connected to healing and deliverance, can take place in any area—finances, children, salvation—anything. Jesus wants to touch every part of our lives. Now, He is not a magic genie so that whenever we ask Him for a miracle or sign He is obligated to give us one. There are, however, times when it is right to ask. Do you need emotional healing? Jesus heals the brokenhearted. Physical healing? Jesus heals all brokenness. Do you need a sign that helps you understand the direction God wants you to take? Jesus can guide you. Are you praying for the salvation of a loved one? Pray and believe that God wants to meet you at your point of need—and sometimes He will do this in a way that supersedes the laws of the natural world.

I am not suggesting that our faith should rest on the miraculous or on signs. Jesus said in Matthew 16:4 that "an evil and adulterous generation seeks after a sign." As I have demonstrated by Scripture, however, neither should the supernatural, including signs, wonders and miracles, be ignored. What we need is balance. We need to know and walk in the written Word, and at the same time know that God is actively and supernaturally involved in our lives.

There was a time in my life when my siblings were enjoying success, but I, their older brother, was riding a bicycle to work as a graveyard dishwasher. A college dropout. Completely vulnerable. Pursuing Jesus and trusting in the supernatural. Today, however, here I am being used by God in a world-wide ministry. There is no other way to explain this. I could never have gotten here on my own; I got here supernaturally. Although I did go back to college to finish my education, the doors that Father God opened for me to get where I am today have been truly supernatural.

I want to encourage you to believe God for the supernatural in your life. Believe that God is personal, that He loves you, that He desires to reveal Himself to you. Expect to experience the supernatural in your life.

PART 3

Moving in the Supernatural

7

Prophecy, Dreams and Visions

The prophet Joel gives us a picture of supernatural experiences we should expect at the end of the age: "It will come about after this that I will pour out My Spirit on all mankind; and your sons and daughters will prophesy, your old men will dream dreams, your young men will see visions. . . . I will pour out My Spirit in those days" (Joel 2:28–29).

By "those days" the Lord was referring to *these days*. How do we know that Joel was referring to these days? Because Peter quoted Joel's prophecy when the Holy Spirit was poured out at Pentecost. Peter declared that all those who receive the Holy Spirit will experience prophecy, dreams and visions (see Acts 2:17–18).

On the Day of Pentecost the believers were gathered together in one place when the Holy Spirit came and filled them. They began to speak in languages they had never learned in order to reach the multitudes, who marveled that these lowly Galileans were declaring the mighty deeds of God in their own tongues. Some mocked them, however, saying they were full of sweet wine.

In the midst of all this Peter spoke up and explained what was happening:

> "These men are not drunk, as you suppose, for it is only the third hour of the day; but this is what was spoken of through the prophet Joel: 'And it shall be in the last days,' God says, 'that I will pour forth of My Spirit on all mankind; and your sons and your daughters shall prophesy, and your young men shall see visions, and your old men shall dream dreams; . . . I will in those days pour forth of My Spirit and they shall prophesy.'"
>
> Acts 2:15–18

Believers should now expect to hear the Lord through prophecy, dreams and visions. I do want to point out that when both Peter and Joel said that old men will dream dreams and young men will see visions, they were not saying that only old men will have dreams or that only young men will see visions. But rather, they were communicating that the Spirit of God is poured out on all people.

I hope you feel excited about this. Maybe, to your knowledge, you have not experienced these supernatural things. Maybe you are hesitating and taking a step back because this is unfamiliar territory. Be assured, this is a real ministry of the Holy Spirit. Not only did God use these three methods to speak to various Old Testament individuals, but He used them to communicate throughout the New Testament as well. For you, as a New Testament believer, this can begin an exciting exploration into the ways that God communicates supernaturally with His sons and daughters.

Before we look at each category specifically, I want to remind you that oftentimes the voice of God is small and quiet. In other words, if you expect every prophetic word, every meaningful dream and every clarifying vision to shake you like an earthquake, you will miss many of them. God can overwhelm you with His presence if He chooses to, but most often He uses subtle promptings.

This is the way the Lord called the young Samuel. The boy thought he was hearing the voice of his mentor in the night and kept running to Eli, thinking he had called. Eli finally realized what was happening and told him to go lie back down and listen because it was the Spirit of God speaking to him.

Scripture confirms, in the story of Job, that we often miss His voice. Elihu was Job's one counselor that the Lord did not rebuke at the end of the book. Listen to the counsel from the Holy Spirit that Elihu gave Job concerning the ways of God:

> "Indeed, God speaks once or twice yet no one notices it in a dream, a vision of the night, when sound sleep falls on men, while they slumber in their beds, then He opens the ears of men, and seals their instruction, that He may turn man aside from his conduct, and keep man from pride; He keeps back his soul from the pit, and his life from passing over into Sheol."
>
> Job 33:14–18

Elihu said that God speaks to us through dreams in order to save us, to rescue us, to direct us, to keep us walking down the path that leads to life. But the problem, he said, is that oftentimes we are not listening: "God speaks once or twice but no one notices in a dream."

In the book of Revelation John wrote, "He that has an ear to hear, let him hear." If we are alert, we will pay attention to the ways in which God may speak to us, including prophecies, dreams and visions. Let me give you an example. I was joining a group of people for a time of prayer, and we were sitting in a circle. A man across from me was just sitting down when I saw in my mind's eye, in the most subtle way possible, a hammer coming down on his head. It was just a wisp of an image; I could easily have missed it.

I said to him, "You know, I just saw a hammer coming down on your head."

He answered me and said, "I found out today that I'm being sued."

Although I initially questioned that what I was seeing was from God, after I told it to him, I knew that the Lord had given him a prophetic word through me. God wanted me to say to him, *I'm with you in this. I understand what you are facing. I know what's going on in your life. I'm going to see you through this.*

This Is for Everyone

Prophecy, dreams and visions are not gifts that God reserves for a select few. No, these are God's means of communication for all. Believe it or not, you have experienced prophecy, dreams and visions. The manifestation of the Holy Spirit at Pentecost confirms this. Think why the Holy Spirit represented Himself as a tongue of fire at Pentecost. Why a tongue? Because it is used for speaking. It indicates that the Holy Spirit's primary purpose with us is to speak to us, and He oftentimes does this through prophecy, dreams and visions. Again, read Joel 2:28–29 and Acts 2:17–18. When you understand the nature of God's communication, you will see how much you experience the supernatural every day.

In this chapter we will look briefly at prophecy, dreams and visions. In the next two chapters you will learn principles to help you become more aware of these means of communication and know what to do with them.

Prophecy

The Hebrew word for *prophecy* is *nebuah*, and it means "bubbling up." Prophecy is the Spirit of the Lord bubbling up to communicate something to you and then giving you the ability to speak it. To prophesy in its most basic form means simply to speak by inspiration of the Holy Spirit.

Many times people prophesy without knowing it. We read in Scripture, for example, that during the days of Jesus, the high priest prophesied and said to the community there, "Don't you know"—speaking of Jesus—"that it is expedient for one man to die for the nation?" The high priest did not make this declaration knowing what he was saying. He did not realize he was speaking a word of prophecy by inspiration of the Holy Spirit (see John 11:49–52).

You also have prophesied and not known it. Let me give you an example. Suppose a friend or a child or a grandchild comes to you looking for counsel, and as you are talking together, some helpful thoughts and ideas come to you. You may actually be prophesying, because sometimes the good counsel that you have been inspired to give is coming to you by the Holy Spirit. And again, prophecy in its most basic form is speaking by inspiration of the Spirit.

91

This does not have to be mysterious; prophecy is real and it is tangible. The thoughts or words "bubble up" from the Holy Spirit within, and you speak based upon the insight and discernment He gives you. You are speaking forth the heart of the Lord by inspiration of the Holy Spirit. That is prophecy. So you see, when both Joel and Peter declare, "Your sons and daughters shall prophesy," that includes you.

Visions

The Hebrew word for *vision* is *chazon*, and it means something seen visually in your mind. Most visions that the Spirit communicates to you are pictures that He places gently in your mind. They are so subtle you could mistake them for your own thoughts.

Again, the Lord can give a dramatic experience in a vision if He chooses to. The vision God gave me of Jesus on the cross was powerful and instantly life changing. Scripture describes some visions that were breathtaking. Isaiah had a vision of the Lord seated on His throne, with the doorposts and thresholds shaking at the sound of the seraphs' voices raised in praise. All he could do was cry out, "Woe is me, for I am ruined! Because I am a man of unclean lips, and I live among a people of unclean lips; for my eyes have seen the King, the LORD of hosts" (Isaiah 6:5). John described seeing the risen Jesus in the book of Revelation, and he fell at His feet as though dead (see Revelation 1:17).

Most visions, however, are not of this nature. Let me give you a recent example. My wife, Cynthia, and I heard someone in our congregation speaking negative, accusing things about another individual. I needed guidance from God as to His will for how to handle this man. Were his concerns legitimate? Was he simply being negative and critical?

As Cynthia joined me in prayer about this, a picture dropped into her mind. It was a picture of the man who was making the accusations, and he was vomiting. This was the guidance from the Lord that we needed. No matter how much the man tried to justify the things he was saying, the spirit behind his words was the work of the enemy. It was for destructive and evil purposes.

Cynthia had discernment about the situation because of a vision God gave her. It was not a vision that knocked her out and laid her on the floor; it was a simple picture that the Lord flashed into her mind. She knew that the Lord was saying to disregard any accusation that brother was making because it was coming from a place of wretchedness. God was saying, *This is not from Me.*

The revelation God gave us through the vision helped us have discernment in terms of how to shepherd that person.

Dreams

When you are awake, God speaks to you through prophecy (He lets words bubble up from His Spirit for you to speak) and visions (He slips pictures into your mind to guide you). When you are asleep, He speaks in dreams. In fact, if you study the Word of God, you will find that dreams are right at the top of the many ways that God uses to communicate with His people. From the beginning of the Old Testament and throughout the New Testament, God uses dreams to communicate His will, purposes and direction. This is a very biblical way of hearing the Lord. Again I want to stress that we are first grounded in the written Word, but dreams should not be ignored.

Note that when Peter quoted Joel saying, "In the last days, [you] will dream dreams," he was not referring to the hope of accomplishing some great thing like getting your dream job or dream home or dream husband or dream wife. Rather, he was talking about literal dreams that the Lord gives you in the night while you sleep in order to communicate with you.

Dreams are the perfect opportunity for the Holy Spirit to get your attention. In the state of sleep, you are not focused on your responsibilities and concerns the way you are when awake. Your eyes and ears are not pulling you this way and that, demanding that you focus on the joys or problems around you or on that which you can see. When you are sleeping, you are not fretting that you have to leave for an appointment in ten minutes. You are not thinking about having supper ready in 45 minutes. You are not stressed to complete a project that is due by one o'clock. You are not listening to someone talk about his ex or her vacation plans. In this sense, when you are sleeping, you are loosed from your connection to the material world. The Spirit can communicate to you in ways that He is not able to use during the day.

Some people say "I don't dream," but we know for a fact that everybody dreams. The question is, Are you in touch with your dreams and are you listening to them? The same can be said for prophecy and visions. Do you notice them? Do you heed them? Since we often miss these three important and frequent ways that God speaks to us, let's study them in further detail.

8

You Can Prophesy

f you are not familiar with the gift of prophecy, I want to begin by pointing out that it is not limited to a certain few. Not only did Joel and Peter state that everyone will prophesy on whom the Holy Spirit is poured out, but additionally Paul wrote that we all should expect this gift: "Desire earnestly to prophesy" (1 Corinthians 14:39). Knowing, then, that prophecy is a good gift that, according to Paul, we should desire, let me share with you some basics.

First let me say that a word of prophecy does not have to be a long message. It would be intimidating to think you have to give a book-length recitation. I recall an incident when a young woman attended our services a few times. She sat toward the back and I had not yet met her. As I was walking out of the sanctuary after one service, I sensed the Lord directing my attention toward her. He spoke one word to me: *Trust*. I felt quiet confidence that it was the Sprit who was speaking, so I went over to her and said, "I feel that the Lord wants me to give you one word from Him for you: *Trust*."

That one word brought her to salvation. I still do not know the depths that the word *trust* reached in her. But the important thing is that it did. God simply used me as He can use you to reveal and impart Himself to those He loves.

This is something any of us can do. No one has to be a theologian to speak one word. We just have to be sensitive, yielded and obedient. What would have happened if I had not believed in the prophetic or was not listening or was not interested to speak to her? Who knows? What I do know is that there has been fruit in her life from my speaking that one simple word from the Lord for her.

Here are four principles to help you grow in your understanding of this gift.

Abide in Jesus

To be able to speak prophetic words, we need first to be grounded in Christ. This is not to say that individuals can never prophesy unless they are deeply grounded in the Lord; rather, in order to live in a place where we can speak consistently by inspiration of the Holy Spirit, we need to abide in Jesus.

I have found in my own life that practicing the discipline of doing nothing in the Lord's presence but simply waiting on Him has sensitized me to His voice. (We discussed waiting on the Lord in chapter 4.) It is difficult to separate ourselves from all our activities and from the things of the world, but in order to get grounded in the Lord and become sensitive to His Spirit, we must do this.

As a practical suggestion, let me encourage you again to take time, preferably an hour first thing in the morning, to spend with the Lord. The way I practice this is to take the first half hour to listen to worship music, songs that are being sung to God. I do nothing but lie before the Lord as I am listening. Then for the second half hour I read and study Scripture and pray.

The discipline of starting out the day by giving the first of our time to the Lord goes a long way in surrendering ourselves to Him, and in so doing we become better able to sense the Spirit's leading in our lives. In short, by giving God the first of the day, we become more in tune with Him and thus are in a better position to hear His voice, sense His leading and prophesy. God will use this time to train us.

Be Bold

To prophesy, we need boldness. We need to step out in faith. Maybe you have sensed the Lord wanting you to say something to someone, but you did not do so because you were afraid—afraid of the person or afraid of being wrong. We will never be able to be used fully by Jesus if we let fear keep us from moving forward. So to prophesy you must be willing to step out and speak what you think God is telling you to share.

It is possible that you come from a background where prophetic words always began with this phrase: *Thus saith the Lord.* Personally I do not like this type of introduction to prophetic words because the one who uses it often assumes too much authority. Many people claim to be speaking a "Thus saith the Lord" word, when in reality it might be a good word but not a God word.

If you are ready to step out, you do not have to begin sharing the word God has given you for someone with the phrase *Thus saith the Lord.* I think a more honest and humble way to share what you think Father has given you for someone is to say to the individual, "I think the Lord wants me to share something with you," and then state the message. Follow this with the question, "Does this make sense to you? Does this resonate with you? Does this mean anything to you?" This allows you to step out in faith without putting God on the hook, because you are not saying, "Thus saith the Lord," but you are simply sharing what you believe God has told you. You are giving the person the opportunity to receive it or not. This takes away a lot of the fear of failure and also protects you from misspeaking in God's name.

It Is Okay to Get It Wrong

The encouragement to be bold does not mean that we can be flippant about the things we share with people. We should take this ministry seriously. We have no excuse to settle for a one-percent success rate or have a hit-and-miss attitude. But, on the other hand, we should not be afraid of failing.

If your heart is sincere, your life is consecrated, and you are truly looking to be a conduit of God's blessing in the lives of others, then you should not be afraid of getting it wrong at times. As Paul said, "We know in part and we prophesy in part" (1 Corinthians 13:9), and that "now we see through a glass, darkly" (1 Corinthians 13:12 KJV). Personally I believe that many so-called mainline prophets today who have prophesied specific things to the Body of Christ that have not come to pass should apologize and admit they were wrong rather than continue to come up with new prophecies without acknowledging the error of their previous ones.

So I take this very seriously. But the general believer, who may be in a position to prophesy, whether it is at home, in a church cell group or at work, who senses that God is giving something to share with somebody, needs to step out in faith, sharing it humbly as I have suggested. I think you will find that oftentimes the person will confirm your word as being authentically from the Lord. The recipient will be encouraged, and you will be blessed.

If the person tells you that the word you gave was wrong or did not resonate, simply apologize—and continue on, because we learn through failing. The more experience you gain, the more precisely you can be used by the Lord in this way. As you have probably heard, it is easier to steer a car that is moving than one that is parked.

Expect Jesus to Use You

Prophecy can be a blessing to the Body of Christ. This is why Paul strongly encouraged God's people to pursue it. Look again at His specific direction to believers: "Desire earnestly to prophesy" (1 Corinthians 14:39).

Let me share with you a recent personal example when someone prophesied in a prayer gathering of about twelve people. I came into the time of prayer having been through a stressful week. You might know that in addition to being the host of the TV program *Discovering the Jewish Jesus*, I also have preaching responsibilities for the ministry and am its CEO. Furthermore, I pastor a church congregation, spend time writing and travel around the world to preach the Gospel. So when I walked into the prayer meeting, I was depleted of my emotional and spiritual resources and energy.

Now I had not shared this with anybody, and my general energy level is pretty high. I think that on the surface no one in the circle would have been able to observe the weight I felt. Then one of our team members spoke up and said, "Rabbi,

I feel that the Lord told me that all of us and this congregation need to hold up your arms by doing more. You have so many responsibilities that we need to be helping you carry some of this load. We need to help you more."

That was such dead-on right word in that moment that I had no doubt in my mind the individual had just spoken a prophetic word of the Lord. I was greatly encouraged by it because it confirmed to my heart that God cares and that He is involved.

This is what authentic prophecy does for the hearers. It lets them know that God loves them, that there is nothing to fear, and that they can face life with confidence, knowing that God is with them and going before them. This is why we should all desire to prophesy—because through it we can bring a significant blessing to others.

There will be times when you find yourself in a position where you want to be a witness to someone, and you need direction as to how to navigate the relationship and what to say. What do you do when this happens? You abide in the Lord and you pray. You say, "Father, open a door for me to share the Gospel with this person. Give me the right words to say." Being in a posture of dependency on the Spirit opens the door for Jesus to work through you, and the Bible says that "the testimony of Jesus is the spirit of prophecy" (Revelation 19:10).

9

Revelation through Pictures

Why does God speak through the symbolic language of dreams and visions? Why not just say what He wants us to know? Granted, there are occasions when the Holy Spirit does speak plainly, such as when Paul saw a vision of a man from Macedonia begging him to come help them. And as a result he went to Macedonia, concluding that the vision was God's direct voice to Him. For the most part, though, God speaks through pictures and words that need to be interpreted.

Take the story of Joseph and his two symbolic dreams, told in Genesis 37. Joseph dreamed first that he and his brothers were out in the field binding sheaves of grain when, suddenly, his sheaf stood up and the sheaves of his eleven brothers gathered around and bowed down to his. In the next dream, the sun, moon and eleven stars bowed down to him.

Joseph's family recognized that these images were symbols of his brothers, his father and his mother. Though they criticized him for seeming to elevate himself to a high position, these symbolic dreams foretold the day when God would exalt Joseph. His family would, in fact, bow down to him.

Through a series of unusual and painful circumstances, Joseph rose in Egypt to the position of second-in-command to Pharaoh, who put him in charge of guiding the nation through a great famine. When Joseph's brothers traveled to Egypt to buy food, they came before Joseph but did not recognize him because he had been living in Egypt for so long. His accent had changed; he had grown up; he looked different. He was in Egyptian clothes and Egyptian makeup.

They bowed low to him, fulfilling the dreams. Joseph revealed himself to his brothers and blessed his entire family with plenty of food and a place to live. The symbolic images shown in the dream truly came to pass.

But the question is, If the Lord wanted to reveal this outcome to Joseph, why not just give him a dream of his family bowing down to him? Why not communicate it straightly and plainly? Why give him a picture of the sun and the moon and the stars?

Let's consider this in connection with the way Jesus ministered through parables. Mark 4:34 tells us that Jesus "did not speak to [the crowds] without a parable." Every truth of the Kingdom of God that Jesus taught, He taught in parables. And what are parables? Symbolic language. In Mark 4, for instance, we read Jesus' story of the farmer who went out to sow his seed and the different types of ground that the seed fell on. Some seed fell along the path, and the birds of the air came quickly and ate it. Some seed fell on stony ground and, because there was no depth, the plants withered away when the sun came out. Other seed fell among thorns, which choked the plants. Some seed fell on good ground and produced good crops.

It was only later, when His disciples came to Him privately and said, "Tell us what You were talking about," that He explained the meaning of the parable. You and I know what the parable means because we have the New Testament to tell us. We have Jesus' words explaining the symbolism, so we understand. But the disciples did not have the explanation. All they had was the parable, the symbolism—seed fell on the ground; some sprang up and withered in the sun; some grew until the thorns choked it out; some was eaten by birds; some grew in good ground. They did not know what it was all about.

So they came to Him privately and said, "What is this?" And Jesus said to them, "To you it has been granted to know the mysteries of the Kingdom of God." As they asked Him for understanding, Jesus explained the symbolic parable to them. So you see, the voice of God often comes to us in symbolic form.

Why would He do this? Consider that as the disciples had to draw closer to Jesus to discover the meaning of the parables, so do we. God speaks to us in symbolic form in order to draw us to Himself and into the process of discovery. When they sought out the meaning of the parable by coming to Jesus for understanding, they grew closer to Him. And so it is today with us.

This is why it is important for us to pay attention to the voice of the Spirit. God is oftentimes speaking to us, but rather than going to Him and asking Him to help us better understand what He is showing us, and thus grow closer to Him as we engage in the process of discovery, some of us instead ignore His voice and let it roll off us like water off a duck's back.

Jesus said, "Seek and you shall find. Knock and the door will be opened. Ask and you shall receive." God does not always make it easy. Most of the time He is going to speak in symbolic language, whether it be through parables, prophecies, dreams or visions. The message is not always going to be straightforward. We are not quite going to know what it means. We will have to go to the Lord and ask Him for understanding.

Revelation of Mysteries

Not only do dreams and visions appear in symbolic form that needs to be interpreted, but they reveal mysteries. Generally speaking, mysteries in the Bible are not truth being concealed but rather supernatural knowledge that the Lord is revealing. So when we speak about a mystery, we are talking about God showing something to us that we could not know on our own. The Lord is revealing something supernaturally that cannot be perceived with our natural senses.

The apostle Paul speaks about this in Ephesians 3:3 when he says, "By revelation there was made known to me the mystery." He was given revelation that explained what would otherwise be unknown. Truth was revealed to Paul by the Holy Spirit through dreams and visions that led him on his journeys and helped him complete his assignments from the Lord.

The same is true for you. The Holy Spirit is unveiling mysteries in your dreams and visions that guide you. He is revealing things to you supernaturally that you could not otherwise know. Are you paying attention?

Warning and Preparation

Sometimes the Lord will prepare you or warn you by showing future events in a dream or vision. Now, in these instances He is not declaring that the particular event He shows you will absolutely come true. Rather, He could be letting you know of a danger so that you can correct your course of action and have wisdom to take necessary steps to avoid it. Or He might be giving you information you need to go through it. We find an example of this in Genesis 15. Abram fell into a deep sleep and the Lord spoke to him, telling him that his descendants would be taken into bondage but come out of slavery with great possessions. God prepared Abraham's family line by giving him a dream about Israel's future.

This foretelling is a biblical concept. We are not joining the ranks of psychics or fortune-tellers; we have nothing to do with them. But on the other hand, we do not want to let fear of the counterfeit stop us from experiencing or receiving that which is authentic and genuine and from the Lord. The Bible is full of examples where God's children have received dreams and visions.

Years ago, back when I was in Bible college, my dog got lost. He was gone for months. I had all but given up on him. Then one night I had a dream that I found him. I woke up and my phone rang: A farmer was calling to tell me he had found my dog. This was not just about the Lord preparing me to receive back what I had lost; He was quickening me to pay attention to my dreams and visions. By speaking to me clearly that I had found my dog—and then when I actually found him immediately after God spoke to me—I began to pay attention to my dreams. He knows the future and wants us to listen for His voice in dreams and visions.

In the dream about my dog, no action on my part was required other than to wake up to the voice of the Spirit. There are instances, however, when God will give you a dream or vision that He wants you to respond to with concrete action. Sometimes you know all at once what to do, and sometimes it is a process of discovery.

The Offer of Encouragement

The Lord will often bring encouragement through dreams and visions. A scriptural foundation for this is Genesis 28:10–16. At that point in Jacob's life, he was running from Esau, who held a grudge against his brother and planned to kill him. In the days that Jacob lived, you could not just move to another city, get on the Internet and make new friends. You were born and spent your life with the same people, in the same area. If you went to a different location, it was because you all traveled together. Although Abraham was called to leave his people, that was a highly unusual event. People did not just leave their roots and go start a new life in another city—that is not the way it was in the ancient world.

So when Jacob's mother heard of the plot, she sent him off to live with her brother until Esau's fury subsided. Jacob had to leave his family, everybody he knew and the place he had grown up. This was extremely traumatic for him. He traveled through the desert all alone, and, I am sure, terrified, lost and lonely. He had no idea what the future held for him.

One night in exhaustion, he went to sleep using a rock as a pillow. He must have been exhausted to use a rock as a pillow! And in that state he had a dream. You probably recall that in the dream he saw a ladder extending to heaven, with angels ascending and descending upon it. God spoke to him in the dream and repeated the covenant He had made with Abraham, Jacob's grandfather. And God promised Jacob that He would watch over him.

When Jacob awoke, he was greatly encouraged. By seeing the angels go up to heaven and then come back down, he now had great confidence. He said, "Surely God is in this place, and I was not aware of it." In other words, God was with him and he did not know it until he dreamed it. Even in his difficult journey he was not alone. Everything was going to be all right.

To disregard your dreams and visions is to disregard the voice of God. I remember a dream the Lord gave me to encourage me in the early years of pastoring our church. It can be difficult to build a Messianic congregation because churchgoers usually think that the services will be uncomfortably different from what they are used to. At that point we held the main service on Friday night, which was a new experience for most people. Others said they hesitated to come because they thought you had to be Jewish, even though most of our congregation is not Jewish. Messianic ministry is challenging.

So in the dream I was ministering in our church. I looked up toward the two glass doors at the rear of our sanctuary where people enter. Beyond those doors in the lobby area, I could see a crowd of people peering into the sanctuary, but they were not coming in—they were only looking. Then I saw a few people begin trickling in. Others joined them and soon a steady stream of people entered the sanctuary. By the end of the dream, there was a strong flow of people coming in, and the sanctuary became full.

I sensed the Lord was telling me, *They're looking in, and they're going to start trickling in more and more. Pretty soon this whole sanctuary is going to be filled.* The Lord encouraged me with that dream just as He did Jacob. And He can do the same thing for you. But you need to be paying attention. Here are suggestions to help you remember and discern the dreams and visions the Lord gives you.

Application Steps

Dreams are often described in Scripture as visions of the night (see Job 33:15; Isaiah 29:7; Daniel 2:19; Acts 16:9). We can also experience visions in the day. Many times, for example, during worship services in the congregation I shepherd, people will see images appear in their minds—images like a waterfall or like a wave rolling over the entire congregation. Sometimes the Lord shows people a vision of something that took place in their lives years ago in order to heal them of a traumatic experience from the past. Whether the Lord gives you a picture in the night or day, these seven practical steps can help you increase your capacity for receiving from Him through your dreams and visions.

Step One: Expect to Have Dreams and Visions

The first step is quite simple: Expect the impartation of dreams and visions into your life. Remember, these experiences are not for a select few. Dreams and visions are about God communicating, and He wants to communicate with all His children. The more you expect them, the more you will pay attention to them and not miss them.

Step Two: Ask to Notice and Remember Dreams and Visions

Because it is easy to miss the visions and dreams that the Holy Spirit gives you, ask Him to help you recognize and remember them. When you wake up in the morning, say, "Lord, did I dream anything last night?" Throughout the day say, "Lord, speak to me." It might take time to begin to develop sensitivity to the ways that God speaks, but if you stay attentive, you will experience more and more the voice of God's Spirit in your life.

Step Three: Plan on Quiet Meditation

We have discussed the importance of giving God the first part of your day and spending time with Him in your prayer room. Remember that Jesus said, "Go into your inner room, close your door and pray to your Father" (Matthew 6:6).

In addition to spending the first part of the day communing with God, you also need to form the habit and discipline of making sure that your heart stays connected to Him. Self-awareness helps you do this. What I mean by this is to monitor where your heart is throughout the day. When you detect through self-awareness that you have forgotten about Father God, you can, by an act of will, redirect your focus and affection back to Him.

Even when you lie in bed at night before going to sleep, you can practice this. Psalm 4:4 says we receive through rest: "Meditate in your heart upon your bed, and be still." How do you "meditate in your heart on your bed, and be still"? When you go to bed at night, before you go to sleep, lift your heart to the Lord. Say, "Lord, I need more of You. Will You strengthen my heart tonight even while I'm sleeping?"

God oftentimes will speak to you and give you revelation or visions during those moments just before you fall asleep at night and in the morning when you are starting to come out of sleep. In the morning, give yourself a few extra minutes to lie in bed awake before you have to get up.

Step Four: Write Down What You See

Get a journal. When you wake up, sit for a few moments and ask yourself, "Did I dream anything?" This might be difficult at first if you are not used to recalling your dreams, but I promise you that if you stick with it, you are going to find that God does speak to you. Not every night, but periodically throughout your life.

You might not know for sure whether or not a dream is from God, but write it out anyway. Be careful to record each dream exactly as you remember it. As you write it down, the Holy Spirit will often bring back other details of what you dreamed. Sometimes you might feel embarrassed by a dream or afraid to write it down because you would rather not face it. Guard against that. Write the dream out exactly as it happened.

Step Five: Ask for Understanding

Ask the Lord to help you understand the dream or vision. Simply say, "Lord, help me understand what this means. Open my heart to hear You." As you write down what you think you are sensing, oftentimes you will begin to have greater insight about it.

At the same time, be careful not to get locked into any one meaning. I have found that I can feel fairly certain about an interpretation, but then days later, even weeks later, the

Holy Spirit will help me understand the images more fully. It is not unusual for the interpretation to be different from what I thought originally. Let the Holy Spirit guide you into full revelation over time.

Also be careful about depending on other people for understanding. The Holy Spirit, who gave you the dream or vision, is the one who will give you the interpretation. Rely on your Father to help you. As God observes that you are serious about hearing His voice, He will give you understanding.

Step Six: Realize That Not All Communication Is from God

Even though dreams and visions are among the most frequent ways God communicates, not all dreams and visions are from God. In fact, most are not. The largest percentage, especially of dreams, is simply the outworking of your mental processes regarding all the different stimuli you have experienced in life. Your psyche may even be processing things that happened years ago. Even though these types of dreams are not directly from the Lord, they can help you know what is going on in your life. If you dream about something that is distressing or disturbing, rather than block it out of your mind, ask yourself, *Why am I dreaming about this?* And then bring it to the Lord. It might be an area where He wants you to take some kind of action that will bring healing, release or freedom. And sometimes just by praying to Him about the distressing dream, healing will come. The point is, rather than run from them, deal with them.

Dreams also can come from the enemy. We all have experienced nightmares that we recognize come from evil, but Satan's attacks upon God's people are not restricted to the extreme of a nightmare. He can attack us through dreams of loneliness, isolation, hopelessness, fear and the list goes on. We live in a world full of darkness—spiritual darkness. That is why Paul said in the book of Ephesians that our fight is not against flesh and blood. We wrestle, Paul said, against principalities and forces of spiritual wickedness. If you are wrestling somebody, you will feel your opponent's strength. The enemy is going to try to stop you from moving forward in the Lord, and that disruption will happen not only when you are awake but also when you are asleep. This is not meant to make you afraid; it is the reality of life.

The Bible says that near the end of time, "Woe to the earth and the sea, because the devil has come down to you, having great wrath, knowing that he has only a short time" (Revelation 12:12). God's people experience the devil's rage. I know I do. Oftentimes when I am making significant strides forward in the Lord, the enemy comes to me in my sleep and tries to bring oppression, torment and distress.

As you move forward on your journey with God to experience the supernatural, the enemy is going to respond. God protects you completely—you are totally secure and safe in Jesus. Yet the Lord also will allow you to experience this war to a degree.

Step Seven: Test the Dream or Vision

Because dreams and visions can come from different places, you need discernment. Suppose you dream or have a mental image that someone you know has evil intentions toward you. Is the Lord giving you revelation to help you live in victory in that relationship, or is the enemy trying to produce fear and distrust in your heart toward that person?

I have found that the devil will often try to bring division in relationships that are important to God's purposes in my life by causing me to have dreams that raise my suspicions about certain individuals. I dreamed once that I was lying in a gutter—completely wiped out and helpless. In the dream, a person that I am close to looked down at me and walked right by. Was this message from the Lord or the devil? When I looked at the dream, I recognized that it did not bear witness with what I know of that person, what I sense about the person, and the history we have together. So I did not allow that dream to cause me to become suspicious, which would have created division—which is what the devil wants to do.

You need to test your dreams. If you are unsure, just say, "God, if this was from You, confirm it to me." Sometimes the Lord might be giving you insight, so take note of dreams. Use discernment and God will confirm. My wife helped me to practice this. There were times when I had dreams that I thought were from God, but I was not one hundred percent sure. Cynthia would help me understand that I do not need to act on it immediately. If I have doubts, I can trust God to confirm it. If you are unsure, continue to ponder the dream or vision. Try not to respond to it until the Lord gives you clarity one way or the other. On the other hand, do not wait if you know you need to act now.

You might want to review your dream/vision journal from time to time because some of the things God reveals to you are not just for a moment; they are guiding principles for your life. The Lord will continue to speak to you through what He has previously shown you. Sometimes, in fact, Father will give you a dream or vision that you write down and then forget about. Then, as time goes on, you may find that that dream or vision is unfolding.

10

Supernatural Healing

Up to this point we have learned the importance of waiting quietly to hear the voice of the Holy Spirit and being receptive. Now we are going to learn to take action in the realm of supernatural healing by building faith. Faith is an action. If you need healing in any area of your life, as a general rule, nothing is going to happen unless you reach out and take hold of it. Action comes before receiving.

This is a challenge for many because they have not settled in their hearts the question as to whether or not it is God's will to heal. They read clearly in the Bible that Jesus heals. But because they have prayed and nothing happened, they are tentative in their approach to believing God for supernatural healing.

How do we reconcile our doubts with the truth of the Gospel? And what do we do when things go wrong? There are answers for these questions. We can walk boldly into the blessed life that Jesus has provided for us—which includes physical, mental and emotional healing. To understand why a supernatural life includes supernatural healing, let's begin with the Jewish roots of our faith.

The Hebrew Roots of Healing

Before we can address healing, we need first to address the forgiveness of sin. The Bible tells us that the only means by which God can forgive sin is through an atoning sacrifice. This means that one who is innocent dies in the place of one who is guilty. The Hebrew people first understood this principle through the event that came to be known as Passover. God's people, who were enslaved in Egypt, were instructed to take lambs without defect, slay them and apply their blood to the doorposts and lintels of their homes. This action, in which the innocent lamb was slain, allowed the angel of death to pass over those homes and not kill the firstborn sons. This Passover event was a foreshadowing of Jesus' sacrifice. This is why John introduced Him at the Jordan River as the Lamb of God (see John 1:29).

After God's people crossed the Red Sea, He led them into the wilderness. Through the many experiences there, God gave further revelation about how sin can be forgiven. Leviticus 17:11 records God's words to Moses: "The life of the flesh is in the blood, and I have given it to you on the altar to make atonement for your souls; for it is the blood by reason of the life that makes atonement." *Atonement* means "reparation, reconciliation, redemption."

Because Jesus made atonement for us, all the graces of God—including healing—are able now to come into our lives. In fact, the basis of healing is the atonement. We noted earlier that the lampstand in the Tabernacle was a symbol of the Holy Spirit (see chapter 1). Likewise, as most believers know, the blood sacrifices of animals were symbolic of Jesus' blood. The sacrifices were "only a shadow of the good things to come" (Hebrews 10:1). They were symbols of Jesus, who was ultimately going to die on the cross and fulfill all that they represented. Because they were shadows that God prescribed, God reckoned them as if they were effective.

Through the ancient sacrificial system, we learn that God's only means of having a relationship with a guilty person was when an innocent animal died and the blood was shed in the guilty person's place. In other words, a guilty person could not be forgiven by performing more good deeds than bad deeds; he or she had still done the bad deeds and was still guilty. I could kiss a thousand people in brotherly love, but if I stab somebody to death, I am still going to go to jail. James 2:10 says, "Whoever keeps the whole law and yet stumbles in one point, he has become guilty of all."

I want you to see here how necessary it was for Jesus to die. The Bible says that "He made Him who knew no sin [speaking of Jesus] to be sin on our behalf, so that we might become the righteousness of God in Him" (2 Corinthians 5:21). He who was deserving of nothing but life ended up being condemned for us. You and I who were deserving of nothing but death ended up receiving life because of what He did for us.

That is why the Old Testament says that He was crushed for our iniquities and that our well-being is a result of what He did for us. This is laid out clearly in Isaiah 52:13–15; 53:1–12, which is the prophetic description of the Messiah. We see Him stricken, smitten of God and afflicted. They pulled out His hair. They pulled out His beard. They beat

Him. They spat on Him. They whipped Him. He took our sicknesses and our infirmities in His own body on the tree. Then a soldier took a spear and pierced His side, fulfilling the prophecy that "He was pierced through for our transgressions" (Isaiah 53:5). This is why Jesus said, "Do not think that I came to abolish the Law or the Prophets; I did not come to abolish but to fulfill" (Matthew 5:17).

But did you know that the Scripture we just noted, Isaiah's words in chapters 52 and 53, speaks of Jesus' death on the cross providing not only for forgiveness of sin but also for healing of our bodies?

Let's take a look at Isaiah 53:4: "Surely our griefs He Himself bore." The Hebrew word that Isaiah uses here for *griefs* is *choli*. *Choli* means "sickness and disease." So Isaiah is literally saying: "Surely our sickness and disease He Himself bore"—meaning that Yeshua took our sickness and disease away from us by absorbing it into Himself. This is why Matthew quotes Isaiah 53:4 as the basis for Jesus healing people. "When evening came, they brought to Him many . . . and [He] healed all who were ill. This was to fulfill what was spoken through Isaiah the prophet: 'He himself took our infirmities and carried away our diseases'" (Matthew 8:16–17).

In His atonement not only did Jesus bear our physical sickness, but Isaiah 53:4 says He also carried away our sorrows. Sorrow is emotional pain. Emotional pain can be some of the deepest pain. Many of us have wounding experiences going back to childhood. Some people have been divorced or have suffered the emotional trauma of a broken trust in an important relationship. And the enemy himself lies to us about ourselves and others, causing emotional pain. Jesus the healer also heals our emotions. This is why Isaiah said

He carried away our sorrows. Praise God! Time does not always heal all things, but—hallelujah!—Jesus can.

Did you know that Jesus is called the *Lamb of God* 29 times in the book of Revelation? He, the innocent Lamb, took our sin and sickness in His own body on the tree. He took our griefs and our sorrows. He carried them away. And because He did, we can be healed.

The focal point in human history was the crucifixion of Jesus, which was authenticated by the resurrection. When God raised Him from the dead, it was God's way of saying, "This sacrifice is accepted for humanity. Whoever believes in Him shall not perish, but have everlasting life." This is why Jesus said, "As Moses lifted up the serpent in the wilderness, even so must the Son of Man be lifted up" (John 3:14). The serpent that Moses lifted up was a symbol of the atonement of Jesus.

Everything hinges on the death and resurrection of Jesus. We must understand that. He had to die so that you and I could be forgiven and healed. If you miss how pivotal this is, then you will not understand the necessity for atonement and the basis for receiving supernatural healing. Jesus fulfilled every requirement in the Hebrew Bible. That is why as a Jewish person I have such unwavering faith. By the grace of God, I see how Jesus completed it all.

Jesus Showed His Authority to Heal

The story of the paralytic told in Matthew 9:1–13 demonstrates that the atonement of Jesus included not just the forgiveness of sins, but also redemption from physical infirmities. When Jesus returned to His own town, some men brought to Him a man who was paralyzed and lying on a mat. The Bible says that when Jesus saw their faith, He said to the paralytic, "Take courage, son; your sins are forgiven."

Note that the first thing Jesus said to the man was that his sins were forgiven. Some teachers of the Law heard this and were appalled that any man would make himself out as one who had authority to forgive sin. They could not believe that Jesus had the audacity to say He could do this—for only God can forgive sin. They said to themselves, *This fellow blasphemes.*

Jesus knew what they were thinking. He said, "Why are you thinking evil in your hearts? Which is easier to say, 'Your sins are forgiven,' or to say, 'Get up, and walk'?" Why did He address both issues of sin and healing? Because both are included in the work He came to do—to bring fullness, restoration, life, comfort, love. He came to bring shalom, which means completeness to both our souls and our bodies.

Now look at His next words. "'But so that you may know that the Son of Man has authority on earth to forgive sins,' He said to the paralytic, 'Get up, pick up your bed and go home.'" Immediately the man got up and went home.

The crowd recognized the authority that Jesus had, and were filled with awe. Nothing like this had ever been seen.

Jesus Healed Everyone

Jesus did not limit His authority regarding sickness, disease and death to certain people. Nowhere in the Bible does Jesus say, "I'm going to heal you . . . I'm going to heal you . . . I'm not going to heal you . . . I might heal you . . . I'm going to think about healing you . . . I'm going to come back to you

. . . I'm going to heal you"—no, we never see that. That is not present in the Word of God. From the beginning of His ministry to the middle of His ministry to the end of His ministry, we see that He healed all who came to Him.

Look at these two Scriptures describing His actions after His baptism and then later in His ministry:

> [Jesus] was going throughout Galilee, teaching in their synagogues and proclaiming the gospel of the kingdom, and healing *every* kind of disease and *every* kind of sickness among the people. The news about Him spread throughout all Syria; and they brought to Him *all* who were ill, those suffering with various diseases and pains, demoniacs, epileptics, paralytics; and He healed them.
>
> Matthew 4:23–24, emphasis added

> Many followed Him, and He healed them *all*.
>
> Matthew 12:15, emphasis added

After His baptism Jesus came out of the wilderness after overcoming the devil and began to minister. And as He proclaimed the Gospel, the first thing He did was to establish the relationship between the forgiveness of sin and the healing of the sick. This is repeated throughout the gospels: "Jesus was going through all the cities and villages, teaching in their synagogues and proclaiming the gospel of the kingdom, and healing every kind of disease and every kind of sickness" (Matthew 9:35).

He was proclaiming the Gospel, which means Good News, and He was demonstrating the nature of the Gospel, the nature of His Person, who He is, what He came to do, showing how great the Good News is by healing everyone who came to Him!

Does God Heal Today?

But what about today? That was then; this is now. Is it inconceivable that this Jesus—who healed all the sick when He walked on the earth, who is now seated at the Father's right hand—no longer heals people? Is it possible that He is not doing it anymore? Many people are still confused about this and question whether or not healing is still for today. Or maybe you are one of those who believe that God can heal, but you are not fully convinced that He *will* heal or that it is His desire to heal everyone.

We will discuss some of the hard questions in the next two chapters—the "what abouts?" What about the person who is not healed? What about demons causing sickness? What about Paul's thorn? For now, let's focus on these truths:

1. One of Father's covenant names is *Yahweh Rapha*, which means "I, the LORD, am your healer" (Exodus 15:26).
2. Jesus said, "He who has seen Me has seen the Father" (John 14:9).
3. "Jesus Christ is the same yesterday and today and forever" (Hebrews 13:8).

If our God is a healing God, if it is His will to heal, would it not *always* be His will to heal? If it is *always* God's will to heal, does that not include today? Right now?

Let this truth sink in: It is God's will to heal. Today. It is not God's will to heal sometimes; it is God's will to heal all the time because He is a healing God. In heaven, "a river of the water of life [proceeds] from the throne of God and of the Lamb. . . . On either side of the river [is] the tree of life . . . and the leaves of the tree [are] for the healing of the nations"

(Revelation 22:1–2). Healing flows from His presence like a river. Healing is always coming from Him. As soon as we touch Him, we are healed. God is a healing God. It is His will to heal, because that is who He is.

What about the Aging Process?

The fact that God wants you whole does not mean that your physical body will not one day die. This is not about getting old. The body does degenerate; that is just part of the aging process. When we meet Him, we will put on new bodies—the mortal shall put on immortality—but in the meantime people's hair goes gray. We are not talking about looking forever eighteen.

But there is a difference between aging and sickness. There is a difference between a tree that reaches its full length of years and dies naturally versus a tree that dies prematurely from blight or root rot or any other disease that kills so many trees.

Everybody dies sometime, but we should picture dying the way Moses died, full of life. Dying the way Abraham died—full of life. Dying the way Joshua and other patriarchs died—satisfied and full of life. They completed the course and one day they simply passed away. There is a difference between that and suffering in agony, in pain and disease. We do not read anything about the fathers of our faith suffering in agony and pain, dealing with festering disease for years before passing away.

Jesus healed the woman who was bent double and said, "Should not this woman, who has been in this agony for these eighteen long years be made whole?" Do you think it is God's will for people to writhe in pain for years and years? I do not think so.

A Remaining Question

Does God use doctors? Some take the position that to trust God prohibits us from looking to the medical community. I think there is a balance. In Colossians 4:14 Paul refers to Luke as "the beloved physician." By Paul's words I think we can assume that Luke was still a physician at the time of Paul's writing to the Colossians. I do not believe that those of us who look to God for divine healing need to be opposed to receiving help from modern medicine or the medical community. My personal viewpoint is that sometimes God heals supernaturally apart from modern medicine, and at other times His healing hand works through the medical community.

In Exodus 15:26 where the Lord reveals Himself as *Yahweh Rapha*, the Lord our Healer, He actually used a tree branch in that incident to sweeten the defiled water of Marah so that the Israelites could drink from it without getting sick (see Exodus 15:22–26). Father God could have just spoken to the water but instead decided to use the agency of some type of tree branch. We have another example when Paul told Timothy in 1 Timothy 5:23 to "use a little wine for the sake of your stomach and your frequent ailments."

Sometimes the Lord may choose to use a natural remedy such as an herb, a prescription medication or a physician. He is sovereign, and He heals the way He wants to in ways that are oftentimes unknown to us. Approximately five years ago I was dealing with a medical issue, and the Lord showed me in a dream to take a combination of herbs, one of which I had never heard of. I obeyed and sure enough I was healed.

Consider Naaman who was the captain of King Aram's army but had become leprous. In response to Naaman's leprosy, the king sent Naaman to the land of Israel where he was directed to God's prophet Elisha in order to be healed. Let's pick up this story in 2 Kings 5:9–11:

> So Naaman came with his horses and his chariots and stood at the doorway of the house of Elisha. Elisha sent a messenger to him, saying, "Go and wash in the Jordan seven times, and your flesh will be restored to you and you will be clean." But Naaman was furious and went away and said, "Behold, I thought, 'He will surely come out to me and stand and call on the name of the LORD his God, and wave his hand over the place and cure the leper.'"

Perhaps you can relate to this; I know I can. Naaman expected his healing to come supernaturally, apart from any intermediary source or action required on his part. He expected Elisha simply to pray, call upon the name *Yahweh*, and wave his hand over him—and then he thought the power of God would fall, and he would be gloriously healed. But instead, the prophet Elisha instructed Naaman to go and wash in the Jordan River seven times. In fact, Elisha did not even talk to Naaman personally; he sent his messenger. Naaman was furious and disappointed. This was not how the supernatural was supposed to work. He expected something more spectacular and dramatic. Naaman's servants had to persuade him to do what Elisha told him to do.

Are we sometimes like Naaman? We expect the sensational—a sudden powerful healing—when at times, Father may choose to heal us in a nondramatic way as in the case of Naaman. Some of us have been waiting for the hand of God to heal us immediately, in one swift, powerful, supernatural wave of His hand over us. But as some of us have experienced after waiting on God for some time to do this without seeing healing manifest, we are eventually directed by the Spirit to go to a doctor. And when we go, the physician directs some course of action, whether it be a dietary adjustment or a prescription, and we recover.

Personally I wish that I never had to use modern medicine for anything. But in my own walk, sometimes the Lord heals me supernaturally without medicine or physicians, and sometimes He chooses to use them. I remember one time I spoke with my physician and told her, "I'm just going to trust the Lord. I'm going to give up all medication."

Her response back to me was, "Well, Rabbi, I feel that the Lord put me on earth to help people like you."

You see, God sometimes wants to teach us that we are dependent on one another. In 1 John 2:27 we read that we have no need for anyone to teach us, for we have received an anointing from the Holy One. Yet we also read in 1 Corinthians 12:28 and Ephesians 4:11 that God has given teachers to the Church. There is a balance. The key is to have God's wisdom and to look to Him.

Think about this. For forty years while Israel was in the wilderness, God provided food for them supernaturally. Every morning they woke up and there it was. God put manna on the ground for them to eat. But as soon as the children of Israel came to the border of the land of Canaan, the supernatural manna stopped, and the Lord provided food for them through the natural means that were in the land—the fruits, vegetables, meats and fish of Canaan (see Exodus 16:35).

The point is that we always need to be looking to the Lord as our source for divine healing. Sometimes He chooses to heal us sovereignly with no agency. Sometimes He may use a natural remedy, modern medicine or a physician. We need to be balanced in our approach, while looking to God at all times.

The Completeness of *Sozo*

Let me ask you a question: How close would you feel to a Messiah who saved your soul but did not care about the pain in your body? How intimately would you be able to connect to Jesus if you believed He opened the way for you to go to heaven but cannot—or will not—do anything about the physical, mental or emotional torment you struggle with every day? Would you be tempted to think that He refuses to help you because He does not care? Would that be a block in your feelings toward Him?

I know in my own life that as I began to trust God for physical healing, I felt much more connected to Jesus. Trusting Him to do something concrete for me in the here and now did wonders for my faith and for experiencing greater fellowship with God. I am presently almost sixty years old, and as I age, health issues have begun to surface. Let me give you an example. I was suffering from irritable bowel syndrome. My stomach was bubbling 24/7 to the point that you could hear it if you were standing two to three feet away from me.

I got sick and tired of looking at my medicine every morning. Once I became convinced that the Lord made the provision for His people for physical healing through the atonement, I decided to step out in faith to believe God for my healing. As I persisted and hung onto God's Word, all the bubbling subsided and the uncomfortable and sick feeling that I had been experiencing in my digestive tract left.

Our God is a God who heals. He is a compassionate God, but we must trust Him. *I am not telling you to stop taking your medicine.* But I do want to encourage you to trust God with your health and His leading as you move forward.

The Greek word *sozo* is a verb meaning "to save, heal, rescue." It is the word that Scripture uses to describe the salvation we have in Jesus. I want you to notice that *sozo* is used to describe redemption from sin as well as healing in our bodies. Let's look at a few examples of this in Scripture.

In Matthew 1:21 we read that Jesus came to "save [*sozo*] His people from their sins." We see the word *sozo* here in relation to Jesus rescuing us from the penalty and power of sin. We accept this concept. We believe that when Jesus died on the cross, He took our sins into Himself and died in our places. That is why we can stand before God holy and blameless. Remember: He who knew no sin, Jesus, became sin on our behalf so that we could become the righteousness of God. We praise God for that!

But, second, notice this same word *sozo* is used in the story of the woman who had the issue of blood and touched the hem of Jesus' garment. "Jesus turning and seeing her said, 'Daughter, take courage; your faith has made you well [*sozo*].' And at once the woman was made well" (Matthew 9:22). Jesus healed her physically. *Sozo*, the original word for *salvation*, is used to show that the ministry of Jesus is both spiritual and physical.

The beloved Scripture John 3:16–17 also uses this word: "For God so loved the world, that He gave His only begotten Son, that whoever believes in Him shall not perish, but have eternal life. For God did not send the Son into the world to judge the world, but that the world might be saved [*sozo*] through Him." In 1 Thessalonians 5:23–24, we read these words from Paul: "Now may the God of peace Himself sanctify you entirely; and *may your spirit and soul and body be preserved complete*, without blame at the coming of our

Lord Jesus Christ. Faithful is He who calls you, and He also will bring it to pass" (emphasis added).

You see, Jesus is a complete healer. He came to save us wholly. Sickness entered the world through sin and is a curse for breaking the Law. But Jesus came to redeem us from both sin and the curse of the Law. Galatians 3:13 says, "Christ redeemed us from the curse of the Law." Because Jesus came to save us from sin and redeemed us from the curse of the Law, there is no reason to remain sick.

The bodies that we have are God's creation. They are God's temples. At creation Jesus looked at the human body and said, "It is very good." God did not create us to live in sickness. And when sickness entered the world because of sin, Jesus came to destroy not only the effect of sin on our souls but also the effect of sin on our bodies. He did not die just to heal our souls; He died to make us whole—spirit, soul and body. When we exercise faith in that, we receive it from Him.

I want to ask you another question. Many people have been taught that they are glorifying God by learning how to be content with their sickness. They hold onto the belief that God will enable them to get through the sickness and endure it. But how much does this glorify God? How much does being sick encourage other people to believe in the God you say loves you? Does being sick in our bodies really bring glory to His name? Jesus said that we should be like lights on a hill, and when people see us, they will have to look up and acknowledge God. We are to be His witnesses that He created good works for us to walk in. How strong a witness can we be, and how many things are we prevented from doing, when we are confined to our homes because of sickness?

The apostle John prayed that we would be in good health (see 3 John 2). If it were God's will for His people to be sick or if healing were only for the time that Jesus walked upon the earth in the flesh, why does God tell us this: "Is anyone among you sick? Then he must call for the elders of the church and they are to pray over him" (James 5:14).

I want to help you get into a place of strong conviction and faith about this. The Bible says that Jesus healed "every kind of disease and every kind of sickness." This is as plain as day. There is not an instance in Scripture where someone came to Jesus and Jesus did not heal the individual. And there is only one instance in Scripture where an individual questioned whether or not it was God's will to heal him, and Jesus responded, "I am willing. Be healed" (see Mark 1:41; Matthew 8:3).

When Jesus died on the cross for you, He died to take away your sin and heal you of disease. He fulfilled what was spoken through Isaiah the prophet that He would take our infirmities, our sicknesses, our brokenness. He took these things unto Himself and carried them away. His sacrifice for your transgressions is the same sacrifice by which you can be healed physically.

In the next chapter, we will begin taking steps for walking in supernatural wholeness. Get ready to put your faith in Jesus in order to receive all that He did for you. Reject completely the notion that it is God's will for His children to be sick their whole lives. Trust that it is Father's desire for His children to be well. Every single one.

11

Walking in Supernatural Wholeness

Now let's put faith into action. As you grow in the understanding that God wants you to experience the supernatural, two things happen. First, you *believe* the Word of God. You become more grounded in its truth. Second, you *receive* the Word of God. Your heart becomes alive with its promises. As you put your faith in God's Word, His power is then released into your life.

This process is not unfamiliar; it is the same way your salvation took place. Romans 1:16 says that the Gospel is "the power of God for salvation to everyone who believes." You accepted—believed—the biblical truth that Jesus died for the sins of the world. Then you received His saving grace for you personally. God's power was then released into your life, and a salvation experience took place. You believed in your heart, you confessed Jesus as Lord, and something supernatural happened.

Learning to put your faith into action follows this same progression. You believe that the Word of God is living and active in believers' lives today; you expect its fulfillment in your life personally; God's power is then released into your heart and mind, and the supernatural is activated in your daily walk.

Get the Full Story

Faith is a substance. Faith is a thing. You take it and use it, and God responds. This is an important concept, and most Christians miss it. They stay almost in a holding pattern, waiting for God to show up and initiate something for them.

Now, listen carefully: I am not negating here the importance of waiting at Jesus' feet to worship and listen for His voice. The time of quiet meditation in your prayer room is crucial for discovering the mysteries of His heart. It begins there. But that is only half the story.

The other half of the story is that God will move in response to your faith. Jesus said, "All things are possible to those who believe." If you are facing a mountain and tell it to move, Jesus said, "Truly I say to you, whoever says to this mountain, 'Be taken up and cast into the sea,' and does not doubt in his heart, but believes that what he says is going to happen, it will be granted to him" (Mark 11:13). If, on the other hand, you never speak in faith, you are probably never going to see big things happen. In order to walk in supernatural wholeness in every part of your life—in order to witness miracles, see the sick healed, cast out demons and change your circumstances by the power of God—you need to use your faith.

In faith the blind Bartimaeus called to Jesus and said, "'Rabboni, I want to regain my sight!' And Jesus said to him, 'Go; your faith has made you well.' Immediately he regained his sight and began following Him on the road" (Mark 10:51–52). To the leper who placed his faith in Jesus for healing, Yeshua said, "Stand up and go; your faith has made you well" (Luke 17:19).

The point in these and many other examples is that Jesus did not randomly pick individuals out of the crowd to heal. Rather, He healed oftentimes as a response to one's initiation of his or her individual faith. Consider the example of the woman with the hemorrhage:

A large crowd was following Him and pressing in on Him. A woman who had had a hemorrhage for twelve years, and had endured much at the hands of many physicians, and had spent all that she had and was not helped at all, but rather had grown worse—after hearing about Jesus, she came up in the crowd behind Him and touched His cloak. For she thought, "If I just touch His garments, I will get well." Immediately the flow of her blood was dried up; and she felt in her body that she was healed of her affliction.

Immediately Jesus, perceiving in Himself that the power proceeding from Him had gone forth, turned around in the crowd and said, "Who touched My garments?"

And His disciples said to Him, "You see the crowd pressing in on You, and You say, 'Who touched Me?'"

And He looked around to see the woman who had done this. But the woman fearing and trembling, aware of what had happened to her, came and fell down before Him and told Him the whole truth. And He said to her, "Daughter, your faith has made you well; go in peace and be healed of your affliction."

Mark 5:24–34

Jesus did not pick this woman to heal. In fact, Jesus turned around after she touched Him and asked, "Who touched Me?"

The disciples' response was, "Lord, look how big the crowd is! There are many people touching You."

But the touch of the crowd was different from the touch of this woman who had just received her healing. Luke describes this same incident and records Jesus as saying, "Someone did touch Me, for I was aware that power had gone out of Me" (Luke 8:46). In other words, the touch of the crowd was just physical. But when the woman with the hemorrhage pressed in with faith, and when her hand of faith touched Jesus' garment as she was saying in her heart, *If I can just touch Him, I will be healed*, then she received Jesus' healing power, and she was made well.

Again let me make the point that Scripture does not tell us that God sovereignly picked her out to heal her, but rather that healing power flows out from Jesus, and that those who connect to Him through faith receive it into their lives.

Do you see the difference? Many of us are waiting for God to act sovereignly, but maybe Jesus is waiting for us to act. If this woman had remained at a distance, far back in the crowd, hoping that Jesus would notice her and heal her, she would not have received her healing. Her faith caused her to press through doubt, to press through unbelief, to press through hopelessness and discouragement, to touch Jesus. And that is what released God's healing into her life.

How do we reach out to Jesus today? The woman in this story touched His garment. We cannot touch His physical robes. So how do we touch Him to receive our healing? Beloved, we touch Him by receiving His Word. His Word has become the "garment" that we must touch—believe in—in order to receive His healing power in our lives.

Application Steps

Jesus loves you from the bottom of your feet to the top of your head. He came to make you completely whole—spirit, soul and body. Here are four action steps to help you walk in supernatural wholeness.

Step One: Make a Right Confession

Your first step for putting faith into action is to confess the Word of God over your life. Scripture says that God's people overcame "because of the blood of the Lamb and because of the word of their testimony" (Revelation 12:11). Making a right confession releases faith for receiving.

Recently I ministered God's healing word to a crowd of several thousand. I made the statement at the end of my ministry that some of them might not be experiencing the manifestation of their healings right at that moment, but as they went home, it would manifest. I said, "You need to believe God's Word that by Jesus' stripes you are healed. Don't confess your symptoms. Confess God's Word."

The next day a man came to me to testify. He said that the night before he could hardly walk without tremendous pain. He had not felt anything instantly after I had prayed for him, but on his way home he was healed completely. He was now able to walk normally. That man stood in faith confessing God's Word and eventually was healed.

Many of us make a mistake when someone prays for us to be healed, or we ask the Lord to heal us and nothing happens immediately. We give up and conclude that God has not answered our prayer. Rather than standing on His Word, we confess that we are not healed. Not all healing is instantaneous. Some people recover over a period of time.

Jesus said at the end of the book of Mark that many who are sick "will recover" (Mark 16:18). Many have forfeited their supernatural recovery because they have placed their faith in their symptoms rather than God's Word.

Never own sickness or disease! Refrain from saying, "Oh, I haven't gotten any help. I still feel the pain." The continuing presence of pain is not the determining factor for your confession. Instead, keep your eyes on Jesus. Speak Scripture. Meditate on the truth that Jesus healed everyone who came to Him. Declare: "Jesus, You took my sickness in Your body on the tree, and by Your stripes I am healed. I am whole, complete, well in my spirit, soul and body. I believe that You were crushed for my iniquities, the chastening for my well-being fell upon You, and by Your scourging, I am healed."

It glorifies Jesus when by faith you receive His promise of wholeness. That makes Him smile. It brings Him great joy and satisfaction. You honor Him when you take a step in faith and confess the Word of God.

I know a woman who was supernaturally healed by her Lord. She was outside one day worshiping Jesus and thanking Him for healing her. She heard Jesus speak to her and say, *Thank you for* receiving *My healing.*

Step Two: Repel Sickness as an Enemy

There is no sickness in heaven. There is no disease. There is no sorrow, sadness or pain. Sickness is an enemy to the Kingdom of God. He wants you to walk in wholeness as you live out His Kingdom here on earth. You can be assured of this because Jesus taught us to pray: "Our Father who is in heaven, hallowed be Your name. Your kingdom come. Your will be done *on earth as it is in heaven*" (Matthew 6:9–10, emphasis added). You can make this even more personal by praying and declaring: "Father, Your will be done on earth, *in my life*, as it is in heaven."

Step Three: Trust That God Has a Plan for Good

In this next step, I want to help you keep moving forward in faith by understanding that God is able to bring good out of every situation. Let's look briefly at the story of Job. Most of us are familiar with his circumstances. The Bible says that Job was the greatest man in all the East. He feared and loved God, and God blessed him—his family, his health, his home, his reputation.

Then one day Satan, the accuser of the brethren, came before God, and God said, "Have you considered My servant, Job?" In other words, God was proud of this one.

Satan said, "You have put a hedge of protection around his entire life. Remove the hedge of protection and we'll see what happens."

So God said, "I'm going to allow you to touch his possessions, but don't touch him."

In one blow after another, Job's children were killed, his property lost. Yet, in all this, Job did not sin.

Once again Satan came before God, and God said, "Have you considered My servant, Job?"

Satan said, "Remove Your hand and let me strike him."

God granted Satan permission to inflict Job with physical sickness. His body was soon covered with boils. Job endured even more suffering when his friends came to console him. Their accusations only added to his horrendous experience. He could not understand what was happening. At the end of the story, we know that God healed Job and restored what he had lost.

Here is what we see: God's purpose was never that Job remain sick. That was a temporary, small slice in the realm of time. It had a function. At the end of the book, Job said, "Before this happened, Lord, before I went through all this, I had heard about You. But now, as I have come out the other end of this thing, now I know You for myself."

Notice also that God did not put the sickness on Job. Rather, He removed His hand. The point is, in everything that happened, God was orchestrating indirectly what was going on. In Hebrew we call God *Adon Olam*, the Master of the Universe. His ways are far beyond our ways. In His sovereignty He can see the bigger picture and accomplish the higher good.

This concept of God using all things to achieve His purposes is also seen in the story of the woman who came out of a life of deep sin that we read about in Luke 7:36–50. Because of her thankfulness for being forgiven, she knelt at Jesus' feet, mingled perfume with her tears and wiped His feet with her hair. The Pharisee who had invited Jesus to dinner watched her and thought, *Get her away—this is too much. This extravagant display of affection and emotionalism is embarrassing.*

But Jesus knew his thoughts and said, "Leave her alone. What she is doing is going to be written about as a memorial." Then Jesus said this: "The one who has been forgiven much loves much. The one who has been forgiven little loves little."

What is the point? The point is that as a result of being saved out of a life of sin, her love for Jesus was actually greater than the love of those who had not experienced such depth of pain. God used her brokenness to produce greater love. Notice that in both the life of Job and in the life of the woman who anointed Jesus with the costly vial of perfume, the Lord used their previous circumstances to accomplish something great, but He did not leave them in their previous conditions. Job was healed and the woman was forgiven.

Step Four: Trust That God Wants You to Prosper

Although many have misused the prosperity concept, nevertheless, it needs to be understood in its proper context in Scripture.

Here again is what John said about the heart of God: "Beloved, I pray that in all respects you may prosper and be in good health, just as your soul prospers" (3 John 2). Is he talking only about the health of the soul? No, he is talking about total health—spirit, soul and body. John said that just as your soul is prospering, so should you expect to be in "good health"—John specifically used the words here, *be in good health*. This is a reflection of walking in the fullness of the Spirit. It is a reflection of the heart of Jesus and what He died to give you.

Did John know the heart of God? I think so. He was the one who leaned his head on Jesus' bosom at the Last Supper and who referred to himself in Scripture as "the one whom Jesus loved."

God is a good Father. He loves you. He wants your soul well. He wants your mind well. He wants your body well. He wants your family well. He even wants your finances in order. It is not God's will for people to live perpetually in debt. How do we know that? Because the Old Testament tells us that God instituted every seventh year to be a year of release and every fiftieth year a Year of Jubilee. On those occasions people were released from their bondage and debts. God's heart wants you to experience freedom both in your finances and in your health.

He says, "Seek first the Kingdom of God, and everything else will be added to you." If you walk in His way, you will have supernatural wholeness wherever you go.

The Word as Living Fire

The Lord spoke to me audibly years ago, and I do not say that lightly. In this encounter I felt fire flowing from God into my soul and then from my soul back to God.

It was like a circle of a living river of fire. As this was happening, He spoke audibly to me in my spirit, and this is what He said: *Seize My Word, and don't let anything else in.*

Beloved, this was not my imagination. It was a powerful encounter with God. And the word He gave me is not just a word for me; it is a word for you, too. Letting any belief other than the truth of the Word of God into your heart will keep you from entering fully into all that God has for you. Going back and forth between doubting and believing will put you into a position of instability, according to Jesus: "The one who doubts is like the surf of the sea, driven and tossed by the wind. For that man ought not to expect that he will receive anything from the Lord" (James 1:6–7). If you believe, Jesus said, and do not doubt, "Nothing will be impossible to you" (Matthew 17:20).

Seize My Word, the Father said to me. And I say to you, seize His Word, and never let anything else in. Take hold of the Word. Believe it and receive it. Do not put your faith in your symptoms or in your circumstances. Keep your trust in God's Word. When you receive the Word—when you put forth your faith actively to receive His promises—then God's power is released into your life. Something supernatural happens. As you exercise faith in His promises, you activate the supernatural and you will ascend into wholeness.

139

12

Dealing with Opposition to Supernatural Living

We have learned that God reveals Himself to His people in supernatural ways. In fact, as we have seen, unless we expect the supernatural, we cannot experience God's power and presence consistently. As we become aware of all the ways His Spirit is working in our lives, we see more of the supernatural.

Unfortunately, this draws the enemy's notice. The devil responds to supernatural people and supernatural acts of God with supernatural opposition. Satan has come to steal and kill and destroy. He wants to sabotage your faith.

In this chapter we will look at key areas where you can expect opposition. This is where you exercise your authority in Jesus' name to overcome the powers of darkness that want to discourage and defeat you, as well as the doubts that might arise in your own heart. As you learn to walk in the freedom Jesus has won for you, you will also need to learn how to fight to keep steadfast in your victory. You can resist the enemy, overcome doubt and hold fast.

When You Have Questions

Here is a beginning principle that will help you keep moving forward when you face opposition. There will be days when you feel that in spite of your prayers, in spite of your growing faith and in spite of your trust in Jesus, things might not seem to be changing. You might think, *You know, I have prayed about this. I have tried to believe God for this. I have faith in Him. But nothing is happening.*

Never let your questions keep you from exercising faith in God's written Word. Does it seem as though God is far away and not close to your heart? Never let your emotions keep you from faith in God's written Word. Jesus died for you out of His heart of love. Hold on to that. Has God promised healing? Is the process to recovery slow? Never let your symptoms keep you from having faith in God's written Word.

The Word of God is sure. Psalm 119:89 says that God's Word "is settled in heaven." We have to remember that God's Word is supernatural; what we see and what we feel is temporary. The enemy will attack us through the sensory realm. Again, Peter walked on water until he saw the waves and felt the wind. As long as Peter stayed focused on Jesus and the Word of God, he was able to stand. But as soon as he was distracted by what he saw and what he felt, he lost the victory. Never allow doubt to come into your heart. Hold fast to God's Word. Jesus is the same today as He was when He walked the earth. He wants you well. Hold on to that.

Some people have questions about Scripture itself—verses they find confusing. As it relates to healing, this is often the case regarding the passage about Paul's thorn in the flesh:

> Because of the surpassing greatness of the revelations, for this reason, to keep me from exalting myself, there was given me

141

a thorn in the flesh, a messenger of Satan to torment me—to keep me from exalting myself! Concerning this I implored the Lord three times that it might leave me. And He has said to me, "My grace is sufficient for you, for power is perfected in weakness." Most gladly, therefore, I will rather boast about my weaknesses, so that the power of Christ may dwell in me.

2 Corinthians 12:7–9

Does Paul's experience give reason enough for allowing pain or sickness to continue, or at least for being ambivalent about seeking supernatural wholeness?

After mentioning the many visions and revelations that he was given by the Lord, including an out-of-body experience of being caught up to paradise, Paul said that because of the abundance of revelations given to him, a messenger of Satan was sent to him in order to keep him from exalting himself. In other words, Paul explained that there was a reason for his suffering—there was a divine intelligence: It was related to the abundance of revelation that had been given to him.

There is a tendency within human nature to become puffed up. Paul concluded that God protected him from becoming puffed up by sending this messenger of Satan to torment him so that Paul would be completely dependent on Him. Paul concluded, "Therefore, I will boast of my weaknesses, for when I am weak, I am strong."

Now that we have established why this messenger of Satan came—in order to keep Paul from being puffed up and to keep him dependent on God—let's focus on who or what this messenger of Satan was.

First, we do not know how this messenger of Satan, this thorn in the flesh, manifested. Was it sickness? The Word does not say. There is much about this passage that is a mystery.

What we do see in Scripture, however, is the use of this same terminology in reference *not* to sickness but to someone who is persecuting God's people.

In Numbers 33:55, for example, God said to the Israelites that if they did not drive out the inhabitants of the land of Canaan, the Canaanites would "become as pricks in your eyes and as *thorns in your sides.*" Then in Joshua 23:13, Joshua warned the people with these words: "[If you make allegiance with the nations, they] will be a snare and a trap to you, and a whip on your sides and *thorns in your eyes.*" In Judges 2:3, the Lord rebuked Israel for disobedience, saying, "I will not drive [your enemies] out before you; but they will become as *thorns in your sides*" (emphasis added throughout).

Never in Scripture does the concept of a thorn in the flesh represent sickness. Rather, the thorns are personalities that persecute God's people. That being so, this is one of the times we make the choice to stand on the foundation that we know to be solid. We know that God's Word is not ambivalent about wholeness. There are no ifs, ands or buts. Either the teaching of Scripture is true or it is not true. Either Jesus died for our wholeness—spirit, soul and body—or He did not. The Word of God is permeated with the healing ministry of Jesus and the supernatural wholeness that came to those who touched Him.

When Sin Leaves You Defeated

Sin will always open the door for powers of darkness to come in and defeat God's people. Sin takes us out from under God's protection and puts us into a realm where we are vulnerable to attacks of all kinds. Listen to the words the Lord spoke to Israel:

"All these blessings will come upon you and overtake you if you obey the LORD your God. . . . But it shall come about, if you do not obey the LORD your God, to observe to do all His commandments and His statutes with which I charge you today, that all these curses will come upon you."

Deuteronomy 28:2, 15

Obedience brings blessing from God's hand; disobedience also has consequences. If we put ourselves into a position where we are not yielded to His kindness and to His tenderness, then sometimes He will allow us to get knocked on our backsides so that we will come to our senses and repent.

Jesus opened my eyes to this some years back. Through my disobedience I walked out from under His protective hand. Just as I was getting ready for a two-week mission trip to Africa, I started having heart pain. I checked my blood pressure; it had shot up. I thought that I had too much to do to slow down. Finally, a few days before I was supposed to leave on my trip, I admitted that I had better go to our doctor. She did an EKG and called me later that afternoon.

"Your EKG did not come back normal," she said. "You need to go in for a stress test."

"Well, actually," I said, "I'm getting ready to leave for Africa—I'm packing right now."

"Rabbi, you need to take your health seriously."

"I have an appointment scheduled with you in about a month," I said. "If it's still showing an abnormal reading, then I'll get the stress test done."

She answered, "I don't think it's going to show a normal reading."

I hung up the phone and had a decision to make. This was a time in my life when I was just beginning to explore divine healing. I saw only two options: Was I going to cling to God's Word or look at the symptoms and cancel the trip? What was I going to do? I made a decision to go forward. I would not take the stress test and would go to Africa as planned. I was going to practice what I was preaching.

By Saturday night, before my flight on Monday, the pain was worse. By three or four o'clock in the morning, I was still awake fighting the pain. Plus, I was getting a guilty conscience. My doctor had just told me there was something wrong with my heart, and I was in terrible pain. I felt irresponsible toward my family. I woke Cynthia and said, "Honey, I can't do it. I can't go to Africa."

When I said that, faith rose up in her heart. She started praying. "Father, I thank You that You are going to use my husband in Africa. I thank You that Your Kingdom is going to be built there."

When I saw her faith, I knew I was supposed to go. I knew it was a supernatural outpouring. So I said, "Well, I guess I am going to Africa." And we both went back to sleep.

When I woke in the morning, I got up to have my devotions. I had just bought a brand-new Bible and had it next to me. Now I will be truthful: I was afraid! I had made up my mind that I was going, but I was terrified. I did not want to wind up in a hospital in Africa. I said, "Lord, I need to hear from You. I need a word. Is this an attack from the enemy? Is this a purely physical issue? Am I missing something? I need a sign if I'm supposed to go."

Very faintly, very gently in my field of conscious awareness, I perceived a picture of a number. Somehow I knew it indicated a page number, so I picked up my new Bible and turned to that page. And do you know what verse my eyes fell on? It was Exodus 15:26. This verse is the only place in the entire Word of God where His sacred personal name *Yahweh* is connected to His covenant with us as our Healer: *Yahweh Rapha.*

I read these words: "He said, 'If you will give earnest heed to the voice of the LORD your God, and do what is right in His sight, and give ear to His commandments, and keep all His statutes, I will put none of the diseases on you which I have put on the Egyptians; for I, the LORD, am your healer.'"

When my eyes landed on those words, they cut me like a knife, right to my heart. It was a sacred moment in eternity for me. It was like sensing that the Word of God is living and sharper than a two-edged sword. I was rejoicing and crying in pain at the same time, because I suddenly understood. Yes, God really wanted me to go to Africa, and was my healer, but I was responsible for some of what I was experiencing because I had not fully trusted Him and had allowed myself to become overly stressed. I was willingly putting myself in too many stressful situations. I was being disobedient to His voice by not slowing down.

The Lord was saying here, *I am Yahweh Rapha. I am the Lord your healer. But you have to obey Me. If you will give earnest heed to the voice of the Lord your God, if you will do what is right in His sight, if you will give ear to His commandments and keep His statutes and His ways, then I will put none of the diseases on you which I have put on the Egyptians.*

Again, I was suddenly deeply grieved about my lifestyle—that I had allowed myself to get sucked into too many details; that I had allowed myself to check my email too many times; that I had allowed myself to be involved in decisions that I did not have to be involved in; that I had allowed myself to enter into conversations that I should just have kept my mouth shut about. I am a very hard worker, but I was creating more work than I needed to do.

I recognized that I had to change the way I was living, the way I was talking, the way I was thinking. I needed to change almost everything I was doing. I needed to make a disciplined, conscious effort to release the stress in my life and create a plan to live in a less stressful way going forward. Though I was cut to the quick by my disobedience, I was also touched and encouraged because I knew that God was telling me, "I am the Lord your healer. I'm going to take care of you. I'm going to protect you. I'm going to sustain you."

And, yes, I did go to Africa and had a powerful crusade. God's Kingdom was built and I was fine.

In this story, the heart pain I experienced was related to my own sin. We see an example of this in Scripture in the life of Jezebel. In the book of Revelation, Jesus spoke to the church in Thyatira about their tolerance of "the woman Jezebel, who calls herself a prophetess" (Revelation 2:20) and who led people into immorality and idolatry. Even regarding this woman, who is the ultimate picture of debauchery and contempt, Jesus said, "I gave her time to repent, and she does not want to repent of her immorality. Behold, I will throw her on a bed of sickness" (verses 21–22).

Because of her persistent sin, God was going to allow the enemy to attack. I believe it was even part of God's design that the enemy would attack. Why? To bring her to repentance. The eternal purpose of God, His heart, was that this wicked woman turn from evil and be brought into wholeness.

Jesus wants us to be aware of any temptation to sin, big or small, that takes us from His heart. David said, "Search me and know my ways. If there be any unclean thing in me, show me." This is an important prayer for believers—one that we should pray regularly. Open your heart to the Holy Spirit. Ask Him to show you any sin in your life that needs to be confessed. Confess the sin and walk away from it.

Be especially aware of the sin of unforgiveness. It will block God's mercy from you. Choose to forgive, whether or not you feel like it. Look at Jesus on the cross and say, "Jesus, because You died for that person who hurt me, I choose to forgive." Take your eyes off the person and just look at Jesus. He died on the cross for the sin of the world. Forgive those who have hurt you. Speak those words of blessing: "Jesus, because You forgave, I forgive."

God is *Yahweh Rapha*, the Lord our healer, but in order to receive His fullness, we need pure hearts.

When the Enemy Tries to Discourage You

Why does God allow the enemy to rise up when you try so hard to move forward? Because the process of continuing to commit yourself to following and trusting Him through the enemy's attack strengthens your resolve. First Peter 4:12 says not "to be surprised at the fiery ordeal among you, which comes upon you for your testing, as though some strange thing were happening to you."

When I decided to trust the Lord to heal me of irritable bowel syndrome, the manifestation of the healing in my body did not take place for several months. During the first couple of months, I continued to meditate on God's Word as it pertained to trusting Him to heal me. The healing came eventually. In retrospect I am glad that His healing did not manifest through my body instantly, because during the months that I resolved to keep hanging onto His Word, my faith was strengthened in a way that it would not have been had the healing happened immediately. In other words, a weight lifter's muscles get bigger as he fights against the force of gravity that he deals with in training. In the same way, challenges are not meant to stop you but to strengthen you. James wrote, "Consider it all joy, my brethren, when you encounter various trials, knowing that the testing of your faith produces endurance. And let endurance have its perfect result, so that you may be perfect and complete, lacking in nothing" (James 1:2–4).

So why does God allow the enemy to resist us when we are moving forward? It is oftentimes meant for our strengthening, for our own good as James said, so that we would become "complete."

There are many examples of encountering the enemy's resistance when stepping out boldly into the supernatural. One example is the individual who decides to go forward with greater boldness in being a witness for Jesus. Suppose she approaches the first person she has ever witnessed to. What happens? She gets rejected and ridiculed. What should she do? Should she go back to her old way of living and stop witnessing, or should she keep her trust in God's Word and continue to go forth? Obviously, you know the answer.

Here is an actual example of what I mean. Several years ago I took a team on a ministry trip. During this trip we were in London for a few days. As you may know, much of the culture in Europe is anti-supernatural. Europe is a continent that, in general, has suppressed God and His Word. Now, while we were in Europe, one young man on our team, who is passionate for God and wanted to be used in prophetic ministry, said to me as we were sitting down for lunch one day, "I think the Lord just gave me a word for that woman sitting over there. May I go share it?"

I nodded, and he got up and walked over to the young woman who was sitting at a table with several other people.

He said, "Excuse me, but I think I might have heard something from God for you. I think your mother or grandmother is a spiritual woman and has been speaking into your life concerning the things of God. Does this resonate with you?"

She looked up at him, not smiling, and said, "No, that makes no sense. Neither one has any faith in God. They are not spiritual people."

My friend came back to us totally humiliated, his tail between his legs. "I don't know what happened," he said. After such a bad start he could easily have stopped trying to share prophetic words ever again.

The next day, Cynthia and I decided to take a walk in the city. We left my friend with two other people on the team and headed out in different directions. We were not able to connect with them all day because of bad phone connections. At about five in the afternoon, Cynthia and I decided to go back to our hotel. Now, London has an intricate train system that is spread out all over the city. As we headed toward the train, we walked right into my friend and the others. I was amazed at this—that with London as big as it is and with no plans to meet up, we all wound up together. I was truly stunned. I knew that God was up to something.

At that point we decided to go into a coffee shop, where I struck up a conversation with a Muslim man at a table right next to mine. He offered me a puff of tobacco from his hookah pipe—which I declined. I prayed silently to find a way to communicate God's love to him and eventually found a way to begin to share Jesus with him. As I was witnessing, my friend spoke up.

Looking at the Muslim man, he said, "Are you struggling with pain in your right knee?"

The Muslim man's eyes got big as saucers. "How did you know that?" he asked.

My friend walked over to stand in front of the man, put his hand on the man's knee and prayed for him. Then my friend told the man to get up and walk around.

The Muslim man was speechless; the pain was gone. He had been supernaturally healed. Looking at my friend wide-eyed, he finally exclaimed, "You must be a holy man!" We continued talking with him and challenged him with the claims of Jesus Christ.

But the point I want to make here is that my friend made a decision to keep going forward after his disastrous first attempt with the woman in the restaurant the evening before. The enemy was challenging his gifting, and my friend pushed back on the opposition and did not give up. He made the decision to try again. His next prophetic word was affirmed, and he was greatly encouraged.

We need to stay focused on Jesus and not let feelings or circumstances stop us. We have to be absolutely convinced of the integrity and truthfulness of God's Word. That gives us the momentum to continue driving forward when the enemy tries to discourage us from supernatural living. It is a law of the universe—physically and spiritually: Darkness will never be able to resist light. John 1:5 says that the light shines in the darkness, and the darkness can never put it out.

Keep pressing forward. Hebrews 10:38–39 says: "My righteous one shall live by faith; and if he shrinks back, my soul has no pleasure in him. But we are not of those who shrink back to destruction, but of those who have faith to the preserving of the soul."

When Dealing with Demons

If you do not take authority over demonic spirits, they will take advantage of you every time, blocking the fullness of supernatural living. Fear, sickness, poverty, lust, greed, hatred—evil spirits of every possible vile identity are looking for opportunities to inhabit people and to make their lives miserable. If you have never understood the victory that is yours in Jesus, if you have never known that you can take authority over spirits of infirmity, fear, depression and sickness, then you are setting yourself up to be a victim. If, on the other hand, you understand the playing field and the authority you have in Jesus' name, you will walk in victory against the forces that are trying to oppose you.

I was ministering in a church recently, and a woman there told me she had epilepsy. She said, "In the times of the Bible they would have said it was a demon." What she meant was that not all illnesses are caused by demons, and that is true. Not every sickness is a demon. Some things that people suffer are simply the result of the natural world that decays, a result of being flesh and blood in a fallen world. Life has a natural cycle: It is birthed; it grows; it dies.

But it is also true that Jesus declared many of the physical problems in the people He healed to be the result of demonic attack. Demons can actually inhabit some particular part of a person's body, inflicting pain. Jesus said it and I believe it. When Jesus cast out the demons, the persons were made well: "A demon-possessed man who was blind and mute was brought to Jesus, and He healed him, so that the mute man spoke and saw" (Matthew 12:22). Notice also that in the case of the crippled woman who was made whole, Satan was identified as the cause of her infirmity:

And He was teaching in one of the synagogues on the Sabbath. And there was a woman who for eighteen years had had a sickness caused by a spirit; and she was bent double, and could not straighten up at all. When Jesus saw her, He called her over and said to her, "Woman, you are freed from your sickness." And He laid His hands on her; and immediately she was made erect again and began glorifying God.

Luke 13:10–13

I want to be clear that I am in no way saying that all sickness is caused directly by demons. On the other hand, Scripture gives us several examples of physical problems whose origin was the realm of darkness.

Supernatural lives attract supernatural opposition. A lot of times before God is about to do something, the enemy comes and does everything he can to stop it. It is just like gravity: You are about to take off in a rocket, and something is trying to hold you down. If you are not aware of this, you might give up. This is not to discourage you! Just the opposite. I want you to see that as you begin putting principles like these into practice, as you press into the Lord, the enemy is going to try to stop you. I remember one time right before I was to start preaching, I suddenly developed a terrible attitude. I mean a really horrible attitude. I was fighting against a foul spirit. But I persevered. As soon as I got up and began to preach, it left and did not return.

Let me tell you about a dream I had that also relates to this. I dreamed that I was in our church out in the lobby area. I was about to go into the sanctuary where about three hundred people were waiting for me to teach them the Word of God. They were hungry and expectant.

Suddenly, a demon began manifesting through a person standing there in the lobby. I looked at the person, took authority over the demon and commanded it to leave. The demon left that person. I was again about to go into the sanctuary when, two seconds later, the demon appeared in somebody else's face. I took authority, cast the demon out, and the demon left. Three seconds later, it appeared in another face.

When I woke, I understood. I was being distracted out in the lobby while the people in the sanctuary were left waiting to receive the Word of God. The devil was going to keep on doing anything he could to keep me from going into the sanctuary and fulfilling God's assignment for me, which was to minister to those who were hungry.

Once you know what is going on, and know the position you hold as a believer in Jesus, you can take authority over those spirits. You can say, "Satan, I reject you—you have no right in my body. I kick sickness out! I kick depression out! Jesus, I have victory in You. I praise You that I am seated with You in the heavenly places!"

This came home to me on the mission field. As I began to grow in my authority in the Lord, demons would manifest in people's lives—particularly in Africa—while I was preaching the Gospel. Although I have seen demons manifest in the United States, I see this phenomenon more often in Africa. I believe the reason for this is that the spiritual roots of America are in the Judeo-Christian faith. This is why, for instance, we have the words *In God we trust* on our currency, and until recently we displayed God's Ten Commandments on government properties. Much of Africa, on the other hand, has its spiritual roots in many forms of witchcraft.

One time, right before I was to go on my next trip to Africa, a friend of mine had a dream. He saw me there with a rhino. At first the rhino submitted to me. It went down on its knees. But then the rhino rose, turned on me in rage, charged and rammed me into a wall. Africa is known for its "Big Five" game animals: lion, elephant, Cape buffalo, leopard and rhinoceros.

I left for Africa a few days later. The first night, the Lord used me to deliver several people from strong demons. The demons manifested in visible ways: The people were rolling on the ground, screaming, foaming at the mouth, their eyes rolled back in their heads. It was just like the stories in the Bible. Jesus set them all free.

The next day I developed severe chest pain. It was so bad I could not hold my Bible up in my hand. In the middle of a training meeting for pastors, I walked over to my associate and asked him to continue the meeting because I thought I was having a heart attack.

Our hosts took me back to the hotel. I hoped that if I could lie in bed, the pain would go away, but it did not lessen. As I was lying there, the Lord brought to my mind the dream my friend had before I left, and how at first the rhinoceros had submitted to me but then turned on me in rage. At that point I realized that I was experiencing the wrath of the devil because of the authority I had taken over him the night before. Once the Lord showed me this, I commanded the demon to leave me in Jesus' name. The heart pain left and did not come back.

You might not encounter demonic spirits raging on the mission field, but that does not mean you will never feel their hatred. You might simply hear confusing thoughts or questions in your mind: *But what about this? What about this?* That is what the devil did to Eve: "Did God really say . . . ?"

If God is leading you in a closer walk with Him and you are experiencing His power and presence more fully in your life, then you are going to have to contend for your freedom.

Perhaps God is leading you to surrender your life in a greater way through tithing, which really is an issue of surrendering the heart. What might happen? Your water heater might break. Your car might need work. Satan wants you to be afraid or distracted and stop the forward momentum you are gaining. Hold fast. If you trust God through the trials, you will enter into greater victory and power. Cling to the truth of Jesus' heart and take authority confidently in His name. Remember, when you move forward in the supernatural power of Jesus, you will encounter supernatural opposition just as He did.

When the Symptoms Come Back

Seeing symptoms return is one of the most significant areas of opposition. You believe that a particular answer is yours, you have begun to walk in wholeness, you are sensing victory—and then the symptoms of the problem come back. We see this frequently with sickness. You gain victory in an area of physical healing—and then a week or two later, it looks and feels as though nothing really changed. Or perhaps you are having victory in a relationship, and then something happens to cause a new break.

How do you process that? Let's make sense of this so you can hold on to your victory. I used to think if the problem came back, the individual was never healed. Now I understand the bigger picture.

Our answer comes in the story of David playing his harp for King Saul told in 1 Samuel 16:23. The Bible tells us that as long as David played, Saul was in his right mind. But after David left, the symptoms returned. Why? Because when Saul was in the atmosphere of worship, he experienced healing.

But because he could not maintain that atmosphere of worship when David left, the problem returned.

In order to maintain the healing or breakthrough that God gives, you need to stay in a posture of thankfulness, faith and worship. Keep thanking God for your answer. Keep cultivating His presence in your life. Also be aware of any lifestyle habits that need to change. If you are watching programs on television that erode your faith, turn them off. If you are hanging around people who are not building you up, make new friends. Keep your eyes on Jesus.

When You Don't Understand

The elephant in the room is the undeniable fact that many believers are not receiving the complete healing that is ours through the stripes of Jesus (see Isaiah 53:5; 1 Peter 2:24).

We have already mentioned that, at times, sickness results from sin, as was the case when the Lord stuck Miriam with leprosy (see Numbers 12), or when Jezebel was cast on a bed of sickness (see Revelation 2:18–20). Another example is when the Lord struck the Israelites in the wilderness with the venomous serpent bites (see Numbers 21:4–9). They were healed as they repented and looked at the bronze serpent that was lifted up on a staff (which was a type of Christ). In these instances, God used sickness for a higher good: to encourage repentance and, in turn, the salvation of the ones He inflicted.

We also learn that sickness is not always the result of sin, as was the case with the man born blind: "As [Jesus] passed by, He saw a man blind from birth. And His disciples asked Him, 'Rabbi, who sinned, this man or his parents, that he would be born blind?' Jesus answered, 'It was neither that this man sinned, nor his parents; but it was so that the works of God might be displayed in him'" (John 9:1–3). In this instance, Jesus said the man's blindness was part of God's plan to glorify Himself.

From the case of Job, who wrestled with the question, *Why am I sick?*, we learn that God uses all things to accomplish something good in the lives of His children (see Romans 8:28). Job's wrestling match with God as he went through his illness ended up bringing him even closer to his Lord. After having come out the other end of a prolonged period of suffering, Job said to God, "I have heard of You by the hearing of the ear; but now my eye sees You" (Job 42:5). Somehow God used this period of sickness in Job's life to draw him closer to Himself.

The point I want to make is that God is by nature a healer. We should believe Him for complete and total healing. But we need to remember that God is sovereign, and His ways are beyond our ways. Why some are healed instantly, some over time, and some not until they go to be with the Lord, I do not know. As Paul said, "For now we see in a mirror dimly, but then face to face; now I know in part, but then I will know fully" (1 Corinthians 13:12).

We all can name people who are trusting God for healing and yet are still dealing with sickness, disease or infirmity. Perhaps this even applies to you. I say to you: Do not give up. Hang on. Cling to God's Word, because sooner or later your healing will manifest. We do not always understand God's reasons or timing. We do understand, however, that God is by nature a healing God, so let's continue to believe Him for supernatural health. And if you are dealing with sickness or infirmity, I speak supernatural recovery over you right now.

When You Want to Give Up

Opposition is meant to wear you down. This means that you will probably not have victory without a fight. Satan has come to steal, kill and destroy, but Jesus said, "Hold fast what you have, so that no one will take your crown" (Revelation 3:11). What does this mean? You contend. You stay rooted in the Word of God. Peter looked at the water. Your situation might not be water—it might be the pain in your leg starting to come back. What are you going to do? Are you going to look at the pain and identify with the pain and confess the pain—and sink? Or is your heart rooted in the eternal, immutable Word of Jesus Christ?

Sometimes healing or breakthrough is manifested instantaneously; sometimes it happens over time. Sometimes it happens over a great length of time. At the end of the day, however, you are healed in Jesus' name. It is going to happen. Never give up! Never accept symptoms as permanent. What is permanent is the Word of God.

Is Satan taunting you? Never give up. Speak boldly: "You're a liar, Satan. Get out of my body." Declare the truth of Scripture: "Jesus, I thank You today that You shed Your blood for me. You died on the cross for me. By Your stripes, I am healed."

When do you do that? Every day. How many times a day? Several times a day. If you are tempted to give up, you confess the reality of God's Word. His Word is eternal. Heaven and earth will pass away, but His words will never pass away. When you resist opposition and hold to God's Word through faith, you will experience the supernatural.

13

· · · · · · · · · · · · · · · ·

His Glory

Whenever God manifests Himself supernaturally to His people—whenever His power or His presence becomes visible in the material world—we experience His glory.

The Hebrew word for *glory* is *kabod*, and it is most often associated with manifestations of God. A lot of times when we think of the glory of God, we probably think of Him exalted way up there in the sky somewhere. Actually, God's glory is most often referred to in Scripture by a physical, earthly manifestation of His power. It most often does not refer to what God is doing up in heaven, but rather to what God does on earth.

Look at Exodus 24:16–17: "The glory of the LORD rested on Mount Sinai, and the cloud covered it for six days; and on the seventh day He called to Moses from the midst of the cloud. And to the eyes of the sons of Israel the appearance of the glory of the LORD was like a consuming fire on the mountaintop."

Jesus said that the "wind blows where it wishes and you hear the sound of it, but do not know where it comes from and where it is going; so is everyone who is born of the Spirit" (John 3:8). We do not see God's Spirit, but we can see the effects of His presence. And when we see the effects of His presence, we are actually seeing a demonstration of His glory. When the Lord appeared to Ezekiel, for example, Ezekiel likened God's glory to a brilliant rainbow: "As the appearance of the rainbow in the clouds on a rainy day, so was the appearance of the surrounding radiance. Such was the appearance of the likeness of the glory of the LORD. And when I saw it, I fell on my face" (Ezekiel 1:28).

God does not always manifest His glory as a rainbow. He has shown it as fire, in a cloud, as a dove—He can manifest His glory in whatever way He wants. The point is that most often in Scripture, when we refer to the glory of God, we talk about Him manifesting Himself in the earth in a way that human beings experience in a tangible way. When His glory is revealed, we encounter Him in power.

But why would God manifest His presence on the earth? Because it is not enough just to believe; eventually God wants us to meet Him. John explained this when he said, "What we have seen and heard we proclaim to you also, so that you too may have fellowship with us; and indeed our fellowship is with the Father, and with His Son Jesus Christ" (1 John 1:3). Paul wrote further, "May [God] give to you a spirit of wisdom and of revelation in the knowledge of Him" (Ephesians 1:17). You see, without true personal experience, all we have is doctrine and religion. Jesus did not come to give us doctrine; He came to bring us into an experience. This is why He described eternal life in this way: "This is eternal life, that they may know You, the only true God, and Jesus Christ whom You have sent" (John 17:3).

Moses understood this. In his famous prayer, "I pray You, show me Your glory" (Exodus 33:18), he was really asking for an experience; he was asking for an encounter; he wanted to meet God. God responded by telling Moses to stand on a rock. When the glory of God approached Moses, God put him in the cleft of the rock and shielded his eyes, but as the glory moved past, God uncovered Moses' eyes and he saw God's back. Moses could not handle seeing the fullness of the power of God's glory, so God dialed it down; He let Moses see the back of His glory. Just as you would plug a transformer into an electrical socket to break down the current for an appliance, so God dialed it down for Moses.

After the Israelites erected the Tent of Meeting, the Tabernacle, "Then the cloud covered the tent of meeting, and the glory of the LORD filled the tabernacle. Moses was not able to enter the tent of meeting because the cloud had settled on it, and the glory of the LORD filled the tabernacle" (Exodus 40:34–35). Notice that in both examples just mentioned God's glory was made manifest when there was a physical expression of His presence on earth.

If Moses and the Israelites experienced this in the Old Covenant, we should expect our faith to lead us to experience it in the New Covenant as well. Not only is it natural to desire this; I believe Father God wants us to desire this. I think it pleases His heart when we desire His supernatural presence. Paul said that God chooses us to make known to us "the riches of His glory" (Romans 9:23). And in Ephesians, Paul prayed for us that we would know God's glory: "I pray that the eyes of your heart may be enlightened, so that you will know what is the hope of His calling, what are the riches of the glory of His inheritance in the saints" (Ephesians 1:18). This is what New Testament faith is about: experiencing the Lord. When we speak about the glory of God or sing about the glory of God, we are not just making a theological declaration. When we sing, "Lord, be glorified," we are asking Him to come and show us Himself.

Jesus was a manifestation of the glory of God. He was God becoming visible upon the earth. He did the same thing for us that God did for Moses. Jesus condescended to let us experience God's glory in a way that we could receive and see. John 1:14 says, "The Word became flesh and dwelt among us, and we saw His glory, glory as of the only begotten from the Father, full of grace and truth." What does that mean? The Word became tangible. We could experience Him, meet Him. It is natural to think about God this way—as a God we experience, a God we meet.

I remember one woman who told me of her encounter with God. She said it felt as though the Spirit of the Lord came to her and dug every wound out of her soul. It was the most painful thing she had ever experienced. She felt as though she would burst. The Lord brought every hurt to the surface and washed it all away. Then she was encased in a bubble of shalom that carried her for days and weeks and even months after. That was an encounter with the glory of the living God—Jesus healing the brokenhearted. God wants to be known.

I pray that your personal relationship with God deepens as you understand your potential to walk in supernatural fullness and behold His glory every day. I pray that you recognize and encounter Him in a new way because you know how much He wants you to experience Him. That is the purpose of this book. To help you look at yourself as a spiritual being who expects to connect with a supernatural God.

Father God is involved intimately in your life. He is performing supernatural signs in order to lead and guide you into supernatural experience. May you be fully saturated with His power and presence—for your wholeness and for the glory of His name.

Let's close with a prayer.

Father God, in Jesus' name, I thank You that You love me and that You are increasing my faith so that I can come into Your presence in a deeper way. Jesus said that God is Spirit, so, Father, I repent right now for trying to understand You and for seeking You only in the natural. I realize that You are above the natural; You are supernatural. From this point forward I set my mind on the things above—where You are. I am open to Your Spirit in whatever way You want to lead me and to show Yourself to me. Thank You that when the Holy Spirit came, He came so that You could speak to me in signs, wonders and miracles, in prophecy, dreams and visions. Thank You that through Jesus I have supernatural healing made available to me. Father, I love You. Thank You for all these things. I pray that You will continue to open my heart. I desire to walk in supernatural glory. Draw me more closely into Your presence. In Jesus' name. Amen.

Study Questions

Chapter 1: The Mystery of the Ages

1. How comfortable are you with the idea of experiencing the supernatural? Does anything about it seem frightening to you?
2. Have you had any experiences that you would consider to be supernatural? If so, what were they?
3. Did you ever look for God in all the "wrong places"? Where did you go? What did you experience?
4. What does it mean to you that the Kingdom of God is within your own heart? Are you comfortable thinking that you are a spiritual being? Why or why not?
5. Which is easier to believe, that God once lived in the Jewish Temple or that He lives in your heart?

Chapter 2: Developing a Supernatural Mindset

1. Why is the marriage of Word and Spirit a crucial safeguard for understanding supernatural experiences?

2. What is your confidence level right now that you are familiar enough with both the Word and the voice of the Spirit to follow supernatural leading?

3. Were you taught as a child that you had to earn God's love? If so, is it hard to change your thinking? If not, what would you say to someone who is stuck in doing works?

4. Does it seem impossible that Jesus loves you just as you are?

5. Which of the four application steps—(1) Come Out from the World; (2) Stop Running; (3) Receive His Peace; (4) Realize That God Wants to Rest in You!—is the hardest for you? Why?

Chapter 3: What God Reveals through the Jewish People

1. Did this chapter change anything about your perspective on the Jewish people?

2. If you are Jewish, do you feel that Gentiles are "equals" according to the Scripture that "in Yeshua there is neither Jew nor Greek"? Is this difficult for you? If you are Gentile, do you have a heart of gratitude that you have been grafted into the vine, or do you feel something different?

3. How often do you pray for the peace of Jerusalem?

4. What have you learned about the faithfulness of God to His chosen people—and how does that apply to you?

Chapter 4: Waiting on God

1. Is your "battery" running low? Why or why not?

2. Are you generally more like Mary or Martha? Why do you think so? If you are a Martha, what do you think of Mary? Do you want to become more like Mary? If so, how could you?

3. What is the hardest thing about making time in your day to wait on God?

4. Once you are actually in your place of prayer, what is the hardest thing to do? Are you willing to make this a daily practice? Why or why not?

Chapter 5: Becoming Spirit-Conscious

1. Would you prefer that God spoke to you like an earthquake or in a quiet voice?

2. Can you think of a time that the Lord spoke to you in His quiet voice? How certain were you that you had heard Him? What was the outcome?

3. Having read thus far, what changes do you see in your ability to hear God's Spirit speaking to you?

Chapter 6: What Are Signs, Wonders and Miracles?

1. Do you feel excited that you can experience signs, wonders and miracles in your life, or do you doubt or lack faith for these types of phenomena?

2. Have you ever received a sign, wonder or miracle from God? What was it? Do you think you are generally hearing His voice? Why or why not?

3. Where do you stand on the continuum between looking for a sign every five minutes on one side and being afraid of them on the other? How does that affect your walk in supernatural experience?

4. If you were going to ask God for a sign about something today, what would it be? How comfortable are you to ask?

Chapter 7: Prophecy, Dreams and Visions

1. The outpouring of the Holy Spirit at Pentecost was a fulfillment of prophecy. Do you consider His being poured out on you personally, with supernatural manifestations, also as a fulfillment of that prophecy? Why or why not?

2. Are you eager to recognize supernatural manifestations of prophecy, dreams and visions in your life? Why or why not?

3. Think of a time that you gave a helpful word to someone. Do you think the Holy Spirit inspired that word?

4. If visions and dreams are subtle messages from God, how likely is it that He is speaking to you in this way? What might keep you from being receptive to these messages?

Chapter 8: You Can Prophesy

1. Have you ever wanted to say something to someone that you felt the Lord might want you to share but been

hesitant to do so? How confident are you that you hear from the Lord clearly and know what He wants you to say to someone else?

2. If you shared a thought or word with someone, and the message was received, how would that make you feel? If it was not received, would that make you hesitant for next time, or would you consider that you had been faithful and leave it at that?

3. How can you encourage yourself to move forward to let the Holy Spirit use you in this way? What excites you about this gift?

Chapter 9: Revelation through Pictures

1. God often speaks to you through symbolism, through pictures that come in dreams and visions. Would you prefer that He spoke plainly? Why or why not?

2. What is the greatest challenge for you in believing that the Holy Spirit speaks to you in pictures? Is the challenge to recognize them? To interpret them?

3. Answer truthfully: Is the outcome of hearing from God worth the effort of recognizing dreams and visions, writing them down, looking for understanding? What does your answer reveal about your desire to experience the supernatural in this realm?

Chapter 10: Supernatural Healing

1. God taught the Hebrew people about atoning sacrifices, which Jesus fulfilled by His death on the cross. Along with our salvation, Jesus paid the price for our griefs

and sorrows, our physical and emotional freedom. Do you agree with this or not? Is this "head knowledge" for you, or do you know it in your heart?

2. Many people struggle to believe that God still heals today. Do you believe that He wants to heal? How does the truth that Jesus is the same yesterday, today and tomorrow influence your answer?

3. Is your faith growing to believe that God heals supernaturally today? Are you being encouraged? If something were holding you back, what would it be?

Chapter 11: Walking in Supernatural Wholeness

1. Supernatural wholeness relies, in large measure, on a walk of faith. God's power is released into your life as you believe His Word and receive its fulfillment. Does this responsibility to partner with God excite you or seem doomed to fail?

2. What do you think God's position is regarding the question of faith? Do you think He is waiting for you to act?

3. To what degree does fear of falling into a "name it and claim it" stance keep you from speaking and trusting that you could receive something good from God?

Chapter 12: Dealing with Opposition to Supernatural Living

1. Any believer who walks in supernatural experience is going to face opposition. Are you willing to keep pursuing God if the powers of Satan and darkness try to stop you? What do you think will be the biggest challenge?

2. Sin is a crucial issue in a walk of faith. How willing are you to let the Lord reveal to you any sin—whether attitude or action—that might be present in your life? If He does reveal something, are you willing to turn from it?

3. Can you think of a time when you resisted the enemy's opposition? Did you feel yourself growing stronger in that instance? How did it turn out?

4. Do you think demons are more likely to harass you in your thoughts or in your actions? Is it easier for you to walk in your authority and repel demons when they come against your mind or when they come against your body?

5. Opposition can take many forms. How encouraged are you to fight back?

Chapter 13: His Glory

1. God's glory is most often spoken of in Scripture when He makes His supernatural presence known in the material world through signs, wonders and miracles. Do you think it is possible for God to perform a sign, wonder or miracle in your life—and you miss it?

2. His goal is for you to be connected in a living relationship with Him. Have you grown in that relationship? How might you grow more?

3. Walking in the supernatural every day is the most natural stance for the believer. Will you pray to Father God right now and ask Him to be glorified in your life?

In 1978, having no concept of or familiarity with Jesus, feeling isolated, unfulfilled and lost, a young Jewish man was suddenly awakened from his sleep. Immediately, a vision appeared to him of Jesus on the cross. "I knew at that instant that Jesus was the answer I had been searching for," says **Messianic Rabbi K. A. Schneider.**

For the first time, he began reading the New Testament, devouring every verse; he says it was like fire to him. He became consumed with knowing and experiencing God, the revelation of His Word and the glory of His Son.

During the past thirty years, Rabbi Schneider has committed his life to a passionate pursuit of Jesus and to being used by God for His glory. Through his years of experience in both personal spiritual warfare and ministry, Rabbi Schneider is able to bring to God's Church deep insight into how to gain victory over Satan and the realm of darkness.

Today Rabbi Schneider hosts the powerful television show *Discovering the Jewish Jesus*, which is available seven days a week in more than one hundred million homes in the United States and approximately two hundred nations worldwide. Viewers tune in regularly as Rabbi Schneider brings revelation on how the Old and New Testaments are integrated, building faith and changing lives.

Several years ago God told Rabbi Schneider, *You are an evangelist.* The fulfillment of this calling is now being witnessed by thousands who attend his crusades across Africa. Preaching to large crowds, Rabbi has seen the truths of God's Word confirmed by the Holy Spirit, with signs and wonders of healings and deliverance.

Rabbi Schneider leads the congregation Lion of Judah World Outreach Center in Toledo, Ohio. He has authored four previous books, *Awakening to Messiah*, *Do Not Be Afraid*, *Self-Deliverance* and *The Book of Revelation Decoded*.

He is a frequent guest on Christian television programs, including *It's Supernatural!* with Sid Roth, *Jewish Voice* with Jonathan Bernis, *Marcus and Joni* with Marcus Lamb and Joni Lamb, and TBN's *Praise the Lord*. He and his wife, Cynthia, have two children and live near Columbus, Ohio.

For more information, please visit his website, DiscoveringTheJewishJesus.com.

More from Rabbi Schneider!

Visit discoveringthejewishjesus.com for a full list of his books.

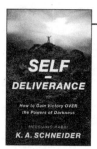

Many of the problems you deal with come directly from the realm of darkness. They are demonic. But this is no cause for fear. In fact, with Jesus' help, you can free yourself! Join Rabbi Schneider as he walks you through every aspect of the biblical self-deliverance process, including how to

- determine which thoughts and actions are inspired by demons
- speak specific commands that force demons to leave
- win against persistent spirits
- close demonic access gained through generational sins, fear and trauma
- experience God's healing presence
- and much more!

Self-Deliverance

"Expect to be set free as you read this book!"
—*Rabbi Jonathan Bernis, president and CEO, Jewish Voice Ministries International*

"Rabbi Schneider unsheathes the weapons every believer must use to win our individual battles against demonic powers."
—*Pat Boone, entertainer and author*

✅Chosen

Stay up to date on your favorite books and authors with our free e-newsletters.
Sign up today at chosenbooks.com.

Find us on Facebook. facebook.com/chosenbooks

Follow us on Twitter. @Chosen_Books